Roll of Thunder Hear My Cry

Novel Literature Unit Study and Lapbook

Unit Study Created by Teresa Ives Lilly

www.hshighlights.com

This unit can be used in any grade level in which students are able to read the book. The activities are best used in grades 2 to 6. Almost everything in the unit can be used to create a file folder lap book. Each unit study covers one whole book and includes:

Comprehension Activities:
Fill in the Blanks, True and False, Multiple Choice,
Who, What, Where, When, Why and How Questions.

Pre-Reading Skills Activities
Author Information Activity, Time line Activity, Theater Box Activity

Lesson Activities
Encyclopedia, Journal, Vocabulary, Sequence of Events, Handwriting
Main Idea, Key Event, Prediction, Comparison,

Literature Skills Activity
Main Character, Main Setting, Main Problem, Possible Solutions, Character Traits, Character Interaction, Cause and Effect, Description, Pyramid of Importance, Villain vs. Hero

Poetry Skills Activity
Couplet, Triplet, Quinzain, Haiku, Cinquain, Tanka, Diamanté, Lantern and Shape Poem

Newspaper Writing Activity
Editorial, Travel, Advice Column, Comics, Society News, Sports, Obituary, Weddings, Book Review, Wanted Ads, Word Search

Creative Writing Activity
Letter, Fairy Tale, Mystery, Science Fiction, Fable, Dream or Nightmare, Tall Tale, Memoir, Newberry Award, A Different Ending.

Writing Skills Activity
Description, Expository, Dialogue, Process, Point of View, Persuasion, Compare and Contrast, Sequel, Climax and Plot Analysis.

Poster Board Activity
Collage, Theater Poster, Wanted Poster, Coat of Arms, Story Quilt, Chalk Art, Silhouette, Board Game Construction, Door Sign, Jeopardy.

Art Expression Activity
Main Character, Main Setting, Travel Brochure, Postal Stamp, Book Cover, Menu, Fashion Designer, Puzzle, Mini Book, Ten Commandments.

Creative Art Activity
Sculpture, Shadow Box, Mosaic, Mobile, Acrostic, Tapestry, Paper Dolls, Book Mark, Photography, Parade Float, Sketch

Other Activities:
Sign Language Vocabulary, Literature Web, Bingo.

How to do the Lapbook Activity: To use this unit study either print out all the pages or Student wills recreate most of them in a notebook or on white or colored paper.

All of the pages can be added to the lapbook project as shown in the photos, or only use those items you want to have students create a lapbook and have them use a spiral notebook for the other pages.

The following are photos of how the work can be presented in the lapbook format. To create the lapbook use 3-6 file folders (colored are best), construction paper or index cards, markers, glue and a stapler.

Front

Back

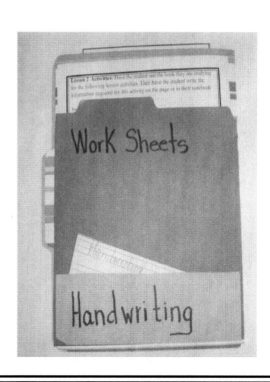

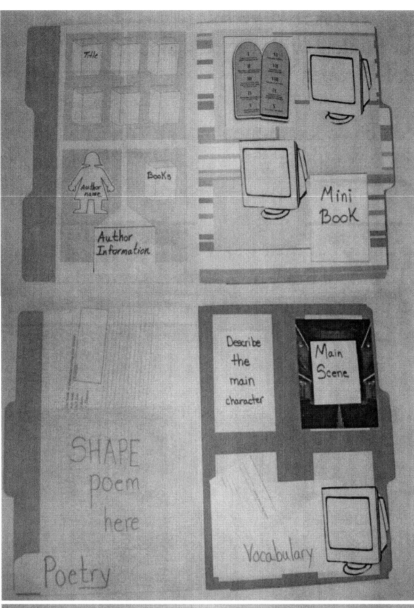

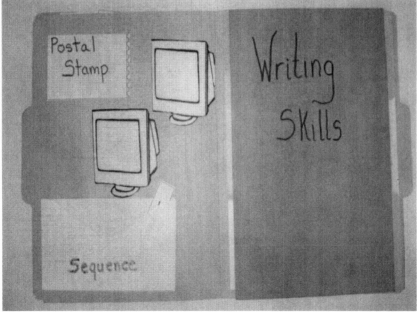

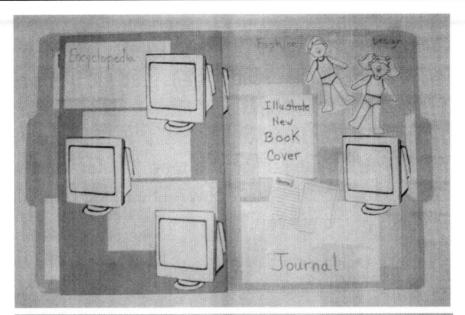

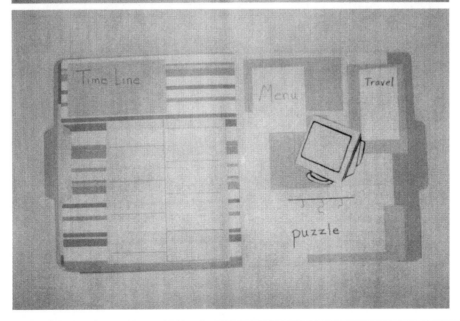

How to do the Newspaper Activity: As the student completes the news paper activities, have student lay the completed work out on a big board or on several poster boards. Don't have them glue the items on the board until the entire newspaper is completed and all sections are put where the student wants them to be. Have student create a name for their newspaper. Then have them type out the name, in big bold letters and place it on the top of the board. with tape or sticky clay. Then tape of stick all the completed articles onto board as well.

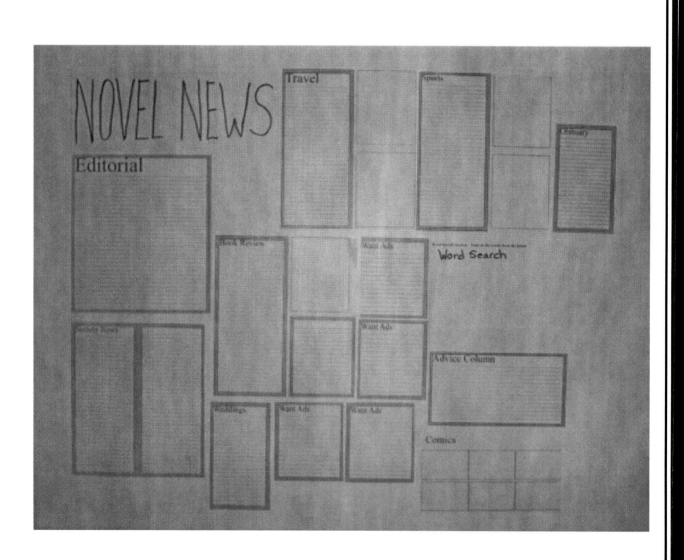

Pre-Reading
Activities

Pre-Reading Activity: Student will look at the book they will be studying for this unit. Then student will write the information required for this activity on the following book patterns or in their notebook. The patterns may be cut out and placed on the lapbook.

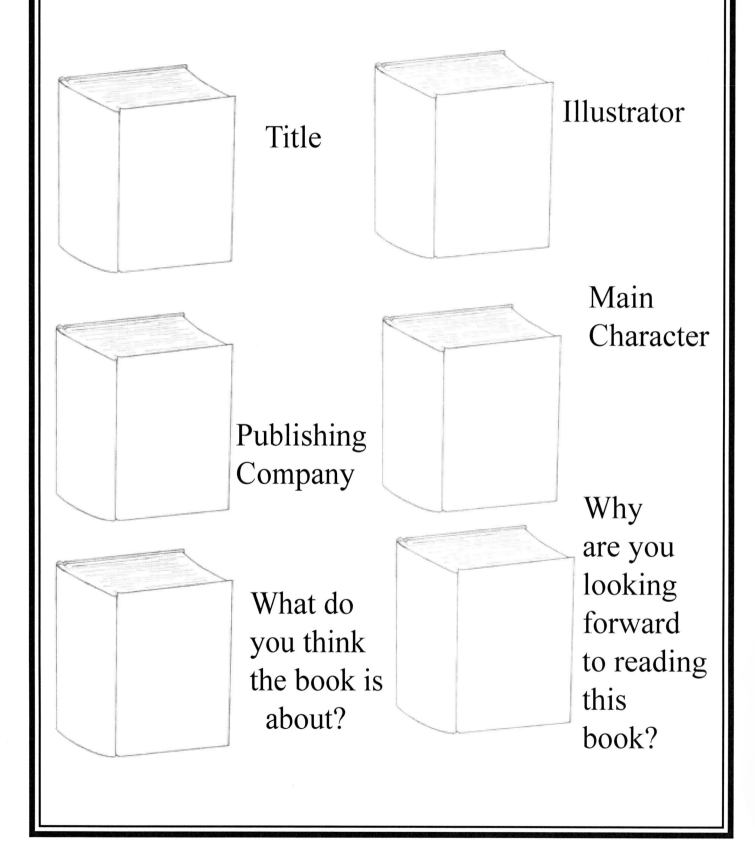

Title

Illustrator

Publishing Company

Main Character

What do you think the book is about?

Why are you looking forward to reading this book?

Author Activity: Student will use the book they are studying and information found on the internet to find out information about the author. Then student will write the information required for this activity on the patterns or in their notebook. The patterns may be cut out and placed on the lapbook.

Student will write the author's name on the correct pattern and the author's age.

Student will rite the name of all the books written by this author on the book pattern. If there are more than three books, just select the three most famous.

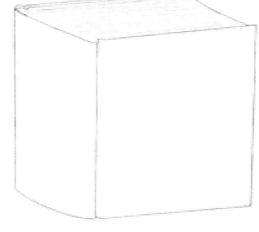

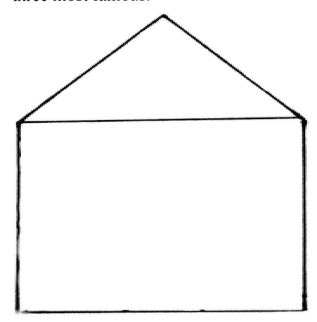

Student will write information about the author on the house pattern, such as where the author was born, lived and how they became an author.

Time Line Activity: Student will use the book they are studying to fill out the time line indicating when anything new, interesting or important happens in the book. This time line pattern can be copied into the student's notebook or this pattern can be printed smaller and placed on the lapbook.

All Vocabulary Lists, Comprehension Questions, True and False, Fill in the Blank for each lesson are at the end of this unit study.

Lesson 1
Activities

Lesson 1 Activities: Students will use the book they are studying and information found on the internet for the following activities. Then the student will write the information required for this activity on the patterns or in their notebook. The patterns may be cut out and placed on the lapbook.

Encyclopedia:
Student will choose one subject from this lesson that interested them and look it up on the internet or in encyclopedia. They will write the name of the subject across the top of the monitor pattern. On the monitor screen section, they will write three or more interesting facts about the subject.

Journal:
Student will imagine that they are one of the characters from the story. After reading each lesson, they will write a short journal entry telling what happened from that character's point of view.
Student will also draw a picture to go along with the journal entry.
At the end of the book, student will staple all the journal entries together to form a complete booklet.
They can even create a special cover for it from construction paper.

Vocabulary word: _____

Definition of the word: _____
_____
_____

Antonym of the word: _____

How many syllables does the word have? _____

Vocabulary Word: _____

Sentence using the word: _____
_____
_____

Synonym of the word: _____

Vocabulary: Student will use the vocabulary words from the list for this lesson. On one of the patterns, or on one index card they will write one vocabulary word. They should also write the definition of the word, then the Antonym and how many Syllables the word has.

On the other card, the student will write the same word. They will write a full sentence using this word and then write the Synonym of the word.

They will repeat this for all the vocabulary words in this lesson.

Place the patterns or cards in an envelope which can be glued into the student's notebook or onto the lapbook..

Sequencing: At the end of the lesson the student will write two of the main events on these two strips. Save them in an envelope which can be glued onto the lapbook or in the notebook. At the end of the book, these strips can be taken out and the student can arrange them in the correct order as they occurred in the story.

Handwriting: Student will pick their favorite sentence that they read in this lesson. Have them write the sentence in their best handwriting on this page or in their notebook.

Student will write out the answers for the following:

Main Idea: In a sentence or two, write what the main idea was of this section.

_____
_____
_____
_____
_____

Key Event: In a sentence or two write what the most important event was in this section.

_____
_____
_____
_____
_____

Prediction: In a sentence of two write what you Predict will happen in the next section.

_____
_____
_____
_____
_____

Comparison: In a sentence of two compare two things in this section. Tell what makes them alike and what makes them different.

_____
_____
_____
_____
_____

Fact or Opinion: In one sentence write a fact about this section and one sentence that is an opinion about the lesson.

_____
_____
_____
_____
_____

Literature Skills: Main Character: Student will write words in the circles to describe the main character.

Physical appearance

Concern or worry

Main character

Who they relate to

Your opinion of them

Poetry Form: Student will write a poem about the book or characters using this format.

Couplet: A Couplet is a two line poem with a fun and simple rhyming pattern. Each line has the same number of syllables and their endings must rhyme with one another. Humor is often used in couplets.

Example:
    If a seed could have its way
    it would grow in just one day.

_____
- -
_____
_____
- -
_____
_____
- -
_____
_____
- -
_____

Newspaper Activity: Student will use this form to write their newspaper piece on then paste it onto their newspaper lay out poster.

Editorial: An editorial is written by the editor of the newspaper. In an editorial the editor gives an opinion of something. Student will imagine that they are the editor of their newspaper. Student will write their opinion of something that happened in the book so far.

Editorial

Creative Writing Activity: Student will use this form or write in their notebook.
Letter Writing: Student will write a letter from one character in the book to another character in the book.

Dear   ,

_____

- -

_____

- -

_____

_____

- -

_____

_____

- -

_____

_____

- -

_____

- -

_____

Sincerely,

Writing Skills Activity: Student will use this form or write in their notebook.

Descriptive: Descriptive writing uses words such as color and texture to describe something. Student will describe a person, place or thing from the lesson.

_____

- -

_____

_____

- -

_____

_____

- -

_____

_____

- -

_____

_____

- -

_____

_____

- -

_____

_____

- -

_____

_____

- -

_____

_____

- -

_____

Lapbook Activity: Main Character: Student will draw and color a picture of the main character on the solid section of the flap book. Student will cut out the entire flap book on the dotted lines and fold the four flap sections over the picture of the main character. On the outside of each flap student will write different words that describes the character; one word per flap.

Poster Board Activity:
Book Collage
Student will print out pictures from the internet that represent characters from the story. They can use magazine pictures as well. Then student will glue these pictures all over a 1/2 poster board in an over lapping fashion to create a book collage.

Creative Art Activity:
Sculpting
Student will create on of the characters from the story out of clay or play doe.

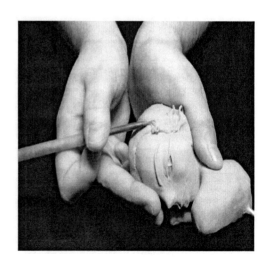

Lesson 2
Activities

Lesson 2 Activities: Students will use the book they are studying and information found on the internet for the following activities. Then the student will write the information required for this activity on the patterns or in their notebook. The patterns may be cut out and placed on the lapbook.

Encyclopedia:
Student will choose one subject from this lesson that interested them and look it up on the internet or in encyclopedia. They will write the name of the subject across the top of the monitor pattern. On the monitor screen section, they will write three or more interesting facts about the subject.

Journal:
Student will imagine that they are one of the characters from the story. After reading each lesson, they will write a short journal entry telling what happened from that character's point of view.
Student will also draw a picture to go along with the journal entry.
At the end of the book, student will staple all the journal entries together to form a complete booklet.
They can even create a special cover for it from construction paper.

Vocabulary word: _____
Definition of the word: _____
_____
_____

Antonym of the word: _____
How many syllables does the word have? _____

Vocabulary Word: _____
Sentence using the word: _____
_____
_____

Synonym of the word: _____

Vocabulary: Student will use the vocabulary words from the list for this lesson. On one of the patterns, or on one index card they will write one vocabulary word. They should also write the definition of the word, then the Antonym and how many Syllables the word has.

On the other card, the student will write the same word. They will write a full sentence using this word and then write the Synonym of the word.

They will repeat this for all the vocabulary words in this lesson.

Place the patterns or cards in an envelope which can be glued into the student's notebook or onto the lapbook..

Sequencing: At the end of the lesson the student will write two of the main events on these two strips. Save them in an envelope which can be glued onto the lapbook or in the notebook. At the end of the book, these strips can be taken out and the student can arrange them in the correct order as they occurred in the story.

Handwriting: Student will pick their favorite sentence that they read in this lesson. Have them write the sentence in their best handwriting on this page or in their notebook.

Student will write out the answers for the following:

Main Idea: In a sentence or two, write what the main idea was of this section.

_____
_____
_____
_____
_____
_____

Key Event: In a sentence or two write what the most important event was in this section.

_____
_____
_____
_____
_____
_____
_____

Prediction: In a sentence of two write what you Predict will happen in the next section.

_____
_____
_____
_____
_____
_____
_____

Comparison: In a sentence of two compare two things in this section. Tell what makes them alike and what makes them different.

_____
_____
_____
_____
_____
_____

Fact or Opinion: In one sentence write a fact about this section and one sentence that is an opinion about the lesson.

_____
_____
_____
_____
_____
_____

Main Setting: Student will fill in the information to describe the main setting and to describe the minor settings in the story.

What is the main setting? _____

_____

Describe it _____

_____

_____

Describe a Minor Setting

_____

_____

_____

Describe a Minor Setting

_____

_____

_____

Poetry Form: Student will write a poem about the book or characters using this format.

Triplet:
Triplets are three-lined poems that rhyme.
Each line has the same number of
Syllables.

Example:
    The bunny hops and hops
    Til all at once she stops
    To munch some carrot tops.

_____

- -

_____

- -

_____

- -

_____

_____

- -

_____

Newspaper Activity: Student will use this form to write their newspaper piece on then paste it onto their newspaper lay out poster.

Travel Section: Student should imagine they write the travel column for a newspaper. Student should write a short article about traveling to the area where this book takes place. Student should find one or two photos on the internet that reminds them of this place and place it on the newspaper lay out poster as well.

Travel

Creative Writing Activity: Student will use this form or write in their notebook.

Fairy Tales : Fairy Tales are fanciful tales of legendary deeds and creatures, usually intended for children. Student will write a fairy tale involving one of the characters from the story and illustrate it.

Writing Skills Activity: Student will use this form or write in their notebook.

Persuasion: Persuasion is a way of writing, in which you convince someone of something. Student will write to try to persuade someone in the story to do something differently than they did in the story.

Lapbook Activity: Main Setting : Student will draw and color the main scene or main setting of this story for a play in this stage scene. Place in lapbook.

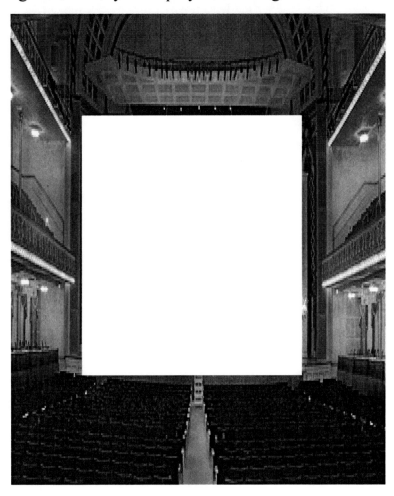

Poster Board Activity:
Theater Poster
Student will create a poster that may be found outside of a theater which is putting on a play of this book.

Creative Art Activity:
Shadow Box:
Student will use a shoe box turned on its side to create a scene from the book in using pictures from the internet or other small items.

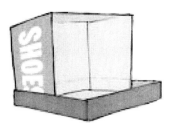

Lesson 3
Activities

Lesson 3 Activities: Students will use the book they are studying and information found on the internet for the following activities. Then the student will write the information required for this activity on the patterns or in their notebook. The patterns may be cut out and placed on the lapbook.

Encyclopedia:
Student will choose one subject from this lesson that interested them and look it up on the internet or in encyclopedia. They will write the name of the subject across the top of the monitor pattern. On the monitor screen section, they will write three or more interesting facts about the subject.

Journal:
Student will imagine that they are one of the characters from the story. After reading each lesson, they will write a short journal entry telling what happened from that character's point of view.
Student will also draw a picture to go along with the journal entry.
At the end of the book, student will staple all the journal entries together to form a complete booklet.
They can even create a special cover for it from construction paper.

Vocabulary word: _____
Definition of the word: _____
_____
_____

Antonym of the word: _____
How many syllables does the word have? _____

Vocabulary Word: _____
Sentence using the word: _____
_____
_____

Synonym of the word: _____

Vocabulary: Student will use the vocabulary words from the list for this lesson. On one of the patterns, or on one index card they will write one vocabulary word. They should also write the definition of the word, then the Antonym and how many Syllables the word has.

On the other card, the student will write the same word. They will write a full sentence using this word and then write the Synonym of the word.

They will repeat this for all the vocabulary words in this lesson.

Place the patterns or cards in an envelope which can be glued into the student's notebook or onto the lapbook..

Sequencing: At the end of the lesson the student will write two of the main events on these two strips. Save them in an envelope which can be glued onto the lapbook or in the notebook. At the end of the book, these strips can be taken out and the student can arrange them in the correct order as they occurred in the story.

_____
_____
_____
_____
_____
_____
_____

Handwriting: Student will pick their favorite sentence that they read in this lesson. Have them write the sentence in their best handwriting on this page or in their notebook.

Student will write out the answers for the following:

Main Idea: In a sentence or two, write what the main idea was of this section.

_____
_____
_____
_____
_____
_____

Key Event: In a sentence or two write what the most important event was in this section.

_____
_____
_____
_____
_____
_____
_____
_____

Prediction: In a sentence of two write what you Predict will happen in the next section.

_____
_____
_____
_____
_____
_____
_____
_____

Comparison: In a sentence of two compare two things in this section. Tell what makes them alike and what makes them different.

_____
_____
_____
_____
_____
_____

Fact or Opinion: In one sentence write a fact about this section and one sentence that is an opinion about the lesson.

_____
_____
_____
_____
_____
_____

Main Problem: Most stories seem to have one main problem. There may be other small problems, but there is an overall large problem. Student will write what the main problem is in the larger rectangle, and some of the smaller problems in the smaller ones.

Poetry Form: Student will write a poem about the book or characters using this format.

Quinzain: Quinzains are unrhymed three line poems that contain 15 syllables. The pattern is: The first line is 7, the second is 5 and the third is 3. The first line makes a statement and the next two lines ask a question about the subject.

Example:
   I like to write poetry
   would you like to write
   a poem too?

Newspaper Activity: Student will use this form to write their newspaper piece on then paste it onto their newspaper lay out poster.

Wanted Ads Section: Student will create several wanted ads that characters in the story might post in a newspaper or ads the characters might answer.

Wanted Ad

Wanted Ad

Wanted Ad

Wanted Ad

Creative Writing Activity: Student will use this form or write in their notebook.

Mystery: Student will write a mystery that may occur in this story or to the characters in this story and then illustrate it.

Writing Skills Activity: Student will use this form or write in their notebook.

Expository: Expository writing is writing strictly to inform. Student will write an expository piece that informs someone about an event that happened in the story.

_____

_____

_____

_____

_____

_____

_____

_____

_____

_____

_____

_____

Lapbook Activity: Travel Brochure: Student will use this form to create a travel brochure on. It should describe a place in the story that people should come to visit. Student may use pictures from the internet if necessary.

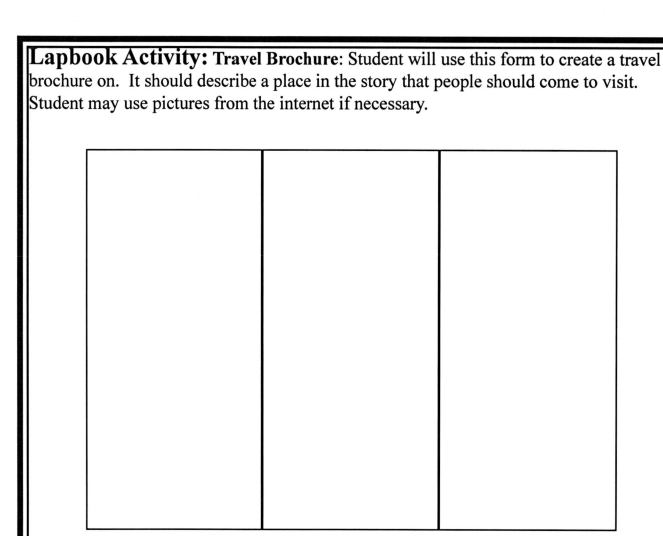

Poster Board Activity:
Wanted Poster
Student will create a "Wanted by the Law," poster for one of the villains in the story.

Creative Art Activity:
Mosaic Plate
Student will create a mosaic scene from the story on a paper plate using small pieces of construction paper glued in a mosaic fashion.

Lesson 4
Activities

Lesson 4 Activities: Students will use the book they are studying and information found on the internet for the following activities. Then the student will write the information required for this activity on the patterns or in their notebook. The patterns may be cut out and placed on the lapbook.

Encyclopedia:
Student will choose one subject from this lesson that interested them and look it up on the internet or in encyclopedia. They will write the name of the subject across the top of the monitor pattern. On the monitor screen section, they will write three or more interesting facts about the subject.

Journal:
Student will imagine that they are one of the characters from the story. After reading each lesson, they will write a short journal entry telling what happened from that character's point of view.
Student will also draw a picture to go along with the journal entry.
At the end of the book, student will staple all the journal entries together to form a complete booklet.
They can even create a special cover for it from construction paper.

Vocabulary word: _____

Definition of the word: _____

_____

_____

Antonym of the word: _____

How many syllables does the word have? _____

Vocabulary Word: _____

Sentence using the word: _____

_____

_____

Synonym of the word: _____

Vocabulary: Student will use the vocabulary words from the list for this lesson. On one of the patterns, or on one index card they will write one vocabulary word. They should also write the definition of the word, then the Antonym and how many Syllables the word has.

On the other card, the student will write the same word. They will write a full sentence using this word and then write the Synonym of the word.

They will repeat this for all the vocabulary words in this lesson.

Place the patterns or cards in an envelope which can be glued into the student's notebook or onto the lapbook..

Sequencing: At the end of the lesson the student will write two of the main events on these two strips. Save them in an envelope which can be glued onto the lapbook or in the notebook. At the end of the book, these strips can be taken out and the student can arrange them in the correct order as they occurred in the story.

_____
_____
_____
_____
_____
_____
_____

Handwriting: Student will pick their favorite sentence that they read in this lesson. Have them write the sentence in their best handwriting on this page or in their notebook.

Student will write out the answers for the following:

Main Idea: In a sentence or two, write what the main idea was of this section.

_____
_____
_____
_____
_____
_____

Key Event: In a sentence or two write what the most important event was in this section.

_____
_____
_____
_____
_____
_____

Prediction: In a sentence of two write what you Predict will happen in the next section.

_____
_____
_____
_____
_____
_____
_____

Comparison: In a sentence of two compare two things in this section. Tell what makes them alike and what makes them different.

_____
_____
_____
_____
_____
_____

Fact or Opinion: In one sentence write a fact about this section and one sentence that is an opinion about the lesson.

_____
_____
_____
_____
_____
_____

Possible Solutions: Problems in a story can have several solutions. Student will write what some of the problems are in the story and possible solution in the shapes.

Problem:

Solution:

Problem:

Solution:

Problem:

Solution:

Poetry Form: Student will write a poem about the book or characters using this format.

Haiku: A haiku is a Japanese poem with no rhyme. Haiku poems have only three lines, each with a certain number of syllables.

Here is the pattern:
Line 1 = 5 syllables
Line 2 = 7 syllables
Line 3 = 5 syllables

Example:
Lion cubs doze in
shade, under shrubs, hidden from
hungry hyenas

_____

_____

_____

_____

_____

_____

_____

Newspaper Activity: Student will use this form to write their newspaper piece on then paste it onto their newspaper lay out poster.

Advice Column Section: Student will come up with a question or concern that one of the characters in the story may have. The student will write a letter to the advice column and the advice column writer will answer.

Advice Column

Creative Writing Activity: Student will use this form or write in their notebook.

Science Fiction: Science Fiction stories take place in the far future usually in space or on earth in an advanced society. Student will write a science fiction story about the future of one of the characters and illustrate it.

Writing Skills Activity: Student will use this form or write in their notebook.

Dialogue: A dialogue is a conversation between two characters. Student will write a dialogue that could occur between two characters in the story. Student should use correct quotation marks.

_____

- -

_____

- -

_____

_____

- -

_____

_____

- -

_____

_____

- -

_____

_____

- -

_____

_____

- -

_____

_____

- -

_____

Writing Skills Activity: Student will use this form or write in their notebook.

Lapbook Activity: Postal Stamp: Student will create a new postal stamp for next year which would represent the book or characters of the book.

Poster Board Activity:
Coat of Arms

Using a poster board, student will create a coat of arms with a design to represent this story or a character in the story.

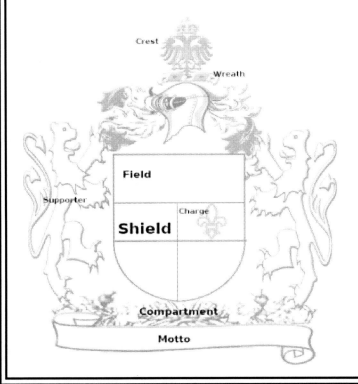

Creative Art Activity:
Mobile

Student will cut out pictures from the internet of characters of items that represent those in the book and then glue them onto long strips of card board. These can be hung with string to make a mobile.

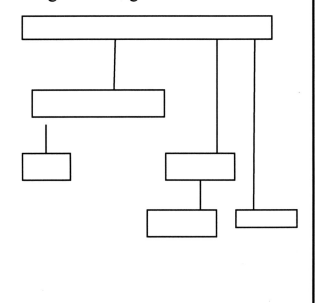

Lesson 5
Activities

Lesson 5 Activities: Students will use the book they are studying and information found on the internet for the following activities. Then the student will write the information required for this activity on the patterns or in their notebook. The patterns may be cut out and placed on the lapbook.

Encyclopedia:
Student will choose one subject from this lesson that interested them and look it up on the internet or in encyclopedia. They will write the name of the subject across the top of the monitor pattern. On the monitor screen section, they will write three or more interesting facts about the subject.

Journal:
Student will imagine that they are one of the characters from the story. After reading each lesson, they will write a short journal entry telling what happened from that character's point of view.
Student will also draw a picture to go along with the journal entry.
At the end of the book, student will staple all the journal entries together to form a complete booklet.
They can even create a special cover for it from construction paper.

Vocabulary word: _____
Definition of the word: _____
_____
_____

Antonym of the word: _____
How many syllables does the word have? _____

Vocabulary Word: _____
Sentence using the word: _____
_____
_____

Synonym of the word: _____

Vocabulary: Student will use the vocabulary words from the list for this lesson. On one of the patterns, or on one index card they will write one vocabulary word. They should also write the definition of the word, then the Antonym and how many Syllables the word has.

On the other card, the student will write the same word. They will write a full sentence using this word and then write the Synonym of the word.

They will repeat this for all the vocabulary words in this lesson.

Place the patterns or cards in an envelope which can be glued into the student's notebook or onto the lapbook..

Sequencing: At the end of the lesson the student will write two of the main events on these two strips. Save them in an envelope which can be glued onto the lapbook or in the notebook. At the end of the book, these strips can be taken out and the student can arrange them in the correct order as they occurred in the story.

Handwriting: Student will pick their favorite sentence that they read in this lesson. Have them write the sentence in their best handwriting on this page or in their notebook.

Student will write out the answers for the following:

Main Idea: In a sentence or two, write what the main idea was of this section.

_____
_____
_____
_____
_____

Key Event: In a sentence or two write what the most important event was in this section.

_____
_____
_____
_____
_____

Prediction: In a sentence of two write what you Predict will happen in the next section.

_____
_____
_____
_____
_____

Comparison: In a sentence of two compare two things in this section. Tell what makes them alike and what makes them different.

_____
_____
_____
_____

Fact or Opinion: In one sentence write a fact about this section and one sentence that is an opinion about the lesson.

_____
_____
_____
_____

Character Traits: In the circle for the Main Character Traits, student will write several of the main character's traits. In the circle for Student Traits, student will write several of the student's traits. Any traits that the main character and the student have in common should be in the area where the circles overlap called Common Traits.

Main Character Traits   Common Traits   Student Traits

Poetry Form: Student will write a poem about the book or characters using this format.

Acrostic: In an acrostic poem the name of the person, object, or place is written vertically down the left hand side of the page. Each letter is capitalized and becomes the first letter of the word beginning each line. The words used should describe the person, object or place in a positive way. Each line may comprise a word, a phrase or a thought that is continued on to the next line.

Example:
CAT
Can you see their eyes
At night in the dark
They glow........

Newspaper Activity: Student will use this form to write their newspaper piece on then paste it onto their newspaper lay out poster.

Comic Section: Student will create a funny cartoon about one of the events of characters in the story. Illustrate and color it.

Comics

Creative Writing Activity: Student will use this form or write in their notebook.
Fable: A fable is a short, allegorical narrative, making a moral point, traditionally by means of animal characters that speak and act like humans. Student will write a fable that comes to mind while reading this story in which one of the characters from the book learns a moral from an animal. Then student will illustrate it.

Writing Skills Activity: Student will use this form or write in their notebook.

Process: Process writing is telling the actual steps it takes to do something. Student will write a step by step process that one of the characters in the book had to do to or should have done.

_____

- -

_____

_____

- -

_____

_____

- -

_____

_____

- -

_____

_____

- -

_____

_____

- -

_____

_____

- -

_____

_____

- -

_____

_____

Lapbook Activity: Book Cover Illustrator: Student will create their own book cover for this story on the form. Make sure to include the title, illustrator and publisher's name.

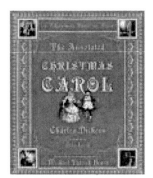

Poster Board Activity:
Story Quilt
Divide a poster board into eight to sixteen equal squares. In each square the student will draw different pictures to tell what has happened in the story so far.

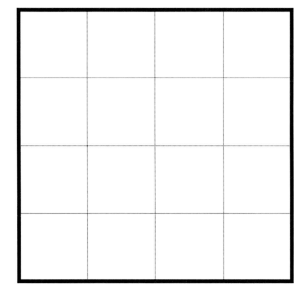

Creative Art Activity:
Tapestry
Using an 8 inch by 12 inch piece of felt as the background, student will cut out characters and items from the story from colored felt and glue onto the background to create a story tapestry.

Lesson 6
Activities

Lesson 6 Activities: Students will use the book they are studying and information found on the internet for the following activities. Then the student will write the information required for this activity on the patterns or in their notebook. The patterns may be cut out and placed on the lapbook.

Encyclopedia:
Student will choose one subject from this lesson that interested them and look it up on the internet or in encyclopedia. They will write the name of the subject across the top of the monitor pattern. On the monitor screen section, they will write three or more interesting facts about the subject.

Journal:
Student will imagine that they are one of the characters from the story. After reading each lesson, they will write a short journal entry telling what happened from that character's point of view.
Student will also draw a picture to go along with the journal entry.
At the end of the book, student will staple all the journal entries together to form a complete booklet.
They can even create a special cover for it from construction paper.

Vocabulary word: _____
Definition of the word: _____
_____
_____

Antonym of the word: _____
How many syllables does the word have? _____

Vocabulary Word: _____
Sentence using the word: _____
_____
_____

Synonym of the word: _____

Vocabulary: Student will use the vocabulary words from the list for this lesson. On one of the patterns, or on one index card they will write one vocabulary word. They should also write the definition of the word, then the Antonym and how many Syllables the word has.

On the other card, the student will write the same word. They will write a full sentence using this word and then write the Synonym of the word.

They will repeat this for all the vocabulary words in this lesson.

Place the patterns or cards in an envelope which can be glued into the student's notebook or onto the lapbook..

Sequencing: At the end of the lesson the student will write two of the main events on these two strips. Save them in an envelope which can be glued onto the lapbook or in the notebook. At the end of the book, these strips can be taken out and the student can arrange them in the correct order as they occurred in the story.

_____
_____
_____
_____
_____
_____
_____

Handwriting: Student will pick their favorite sentence they read in this lesson. Have them write the sentence in their best handwriting on this page or in their notebook.

Student will write out the answers for the following:

Main Idea: In a sentence or two, write what the main idea was of this section.

_____
_____
_____
_____
_____
_____
_____

Key Event: In a sentence or two write what the most important event was in this section.

_____
_____
_____
_____
_____
_____
_____

Prediction: In a sentence of two write what you Predict will happen in the next section.

_____
_____
_____
_____
_____
_____
_____

Comparison: In a sentence of two compare two things in this section. Tell what makes them alike and what makes them different.

_____
_____
_____
_____
_____
_____

Fact or Opinion: In one sentence write a fact about this section and one sentence that is an opinion about the lesson.

_____
_____
_____
_____
_____
_____

Character Interaction:
In the circles, student will write the names of the characters in the story and then draw arrows from each circle to other circles to represent which character interact with one another. Start with the Main Character in the center.

Poetry Form:
Student will write a poem about the book or characters using this format.

Cinquain: A cinquain is a short, five-line, non rhyming poem which follows the following pattern:

First line - The title (one word)
2nd line - Describes the title (two words)
3rd line - Express action (three words)
4th line - A feeling or thought (four words)
5th line - A Synonym or close word for the title

Example:
Insect
six legs
usually have wings
a mostly helpful annoyance
Bee

Newspaper Activity: Student will use this form to write their newspaper piece on then paste it onto their newspaper lay out poster.

Obituary Section: Student will imagine that one or more of the characters in the book died and will write an obituary telling how they died.

Wedding Announcement Section: Student will imagine that one of the characters in the story will get married soon and will write the wedding announcement, telling who they will marry, where and when the wedding will take place.

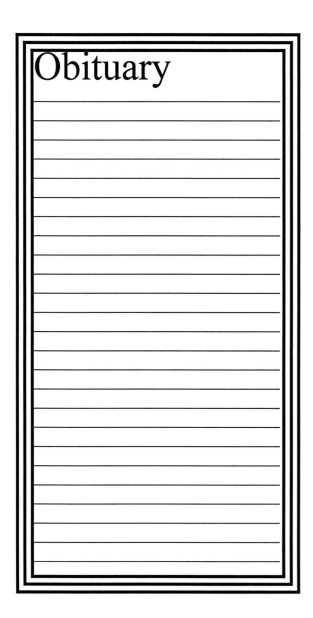

Obituary

Weddings

Creative Writing Activity: Dream or Nightmare: Student will write a dream or nightmare one of the characters in the story may have, and illustrate it.

Writing Skills Activity: Student will use this form or write in their notebook.

Point of View: Point of View is telling a story from one person's view. Student will write about an event in this story from a different character's point of view.

_____

_____

_____

_____

_____

_____

_____

_____

_____

_____

_____

_____

_____

_____

_____

_____

_____

_____

_____

_____

_____

_____

_____

_____

_____

_____

_____

Lapbook Activity: Menu: Student will create a menu for a restaurant that the characters in the book may have owned or eaten at. Student will decorate the front of the menu in an interesting and inviting fashion.

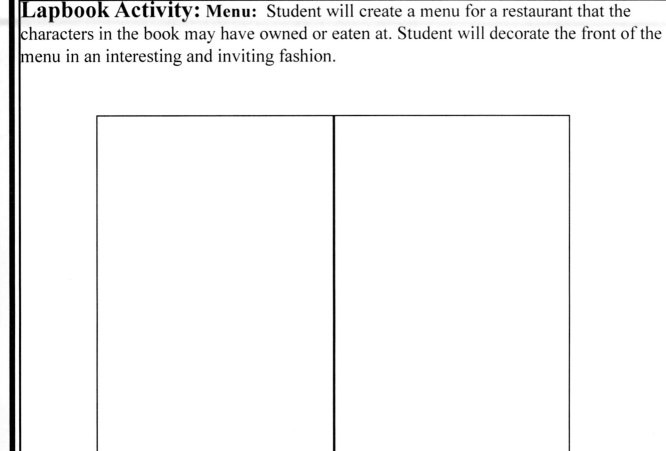

Poster Board Activity:
Chalk Art
On a black poster board student will use colored chalk to illustrate a scene or event in the story.

Creative Art Activity:
Paper Doll
Student will cut out pictures from the internet of people to represent the characters in this story and then laminate them and glue them onto sticks. Students can use them to act out parts of the story or the dialogue the student wrote in an earlier lesson.

Lesson 7
Activities

Lesson 7 Activities: Students will use the book they are studying and information found on the internet for the following activities. Then the student will write the information required for this activity on the patterns or in their notebook. The patterns may be cut out and placed on the lapbook.

Encyclopedia:
Student will choose one subject from this lesson that interested them and look it up on the internet or in encyclopedia. They will write the name of the subject across the top of the monitor pattern. On the monitor screen section, they will write three or more interesting facts about the subject.

Journal:
Student will imagine that they are one of the characters from the story. After reading each lesson, they will write a short journal entry telling what happened from that character's point of view.
Student will also draw a picture to go along with the journal entry.
At the end of the book, student will staple all the journal entries together to form a complete booklet.
They can even create a special cover for it from construction paper.

Vocabulary word: _____
Definition of the word: _____
_____
_____

Antonym of the word: _____
How many syllables does the word have? _____

Vocabulary Word: _____
Sentence using the word: _____
_____
_____

Synonym of the word: _____

Vocabulary: Student will use the vocabulary words from the list for this lesson. On one of the patterns, or on one index card they will write one vocabulary word. They should also write the definition of the word, then the Antonym and how many Syllables the word has.

On the other card, the student will write the same word. They will write a full sentence using this word and then write the Synonym of the word.

They will repeat this for all the vocabulary words in this lesson.

Place the patterns or cards in an envelope which can be glued into the student's notebook or onto the lapbook..

Sequencing: At the end of the lesson the student will write two of the main events on these two strips. Save them in an envelope which can be glued onto the lapbook or in the notebook. At the end of the book, these strips can be taken out and the student can arrange them in the correct order as they occurred in the story.

_____
_____
_____
_____
_____
_____
_____

Handwriting: Student will pick their favorite sentence that they read in this lesson. Have them write the sentence in their best handwriting on this page or in their notebook.

Student will write out the answers for the following:

Main Idea: In a sentence or two, write what the main idea was of this section.

_____
_____
_____
_____
_____
_____

Key Event: In a sentence or two write what the most important event was in this section.

_____
_____
_____
_____
_____
_____

Prediction: In a sentence of two write what you Predict will happen in the next section.

_____
_____
_____
_____
_____
_____

Comparison: In a sentence of two compare two things in this section. Tell what makes them alike and what makes them different.

_____
_____
_____
_____
_____

Fact or Opinion: In one sentence write a fact about this section and one sentence that is an opinion about the lesson.

_____
_____
_____
_____
_____

Cause and Effect: When one thing happens in a story, many other things happen because of this one event. This is called cause and effect. In the center circle, student will write one thing that happened in the story (the cause). In the smaller circles, student will write the variety of things that happened because of that main cause (the effects).

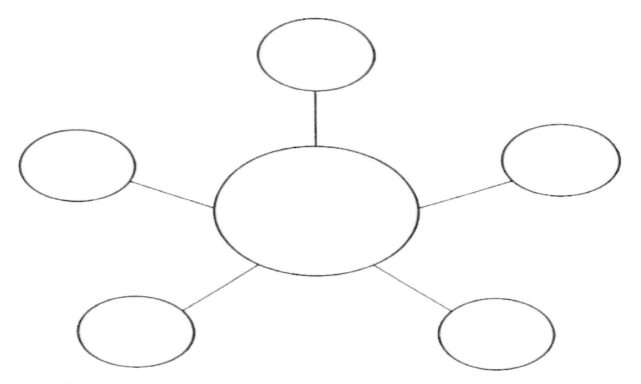

Poetry Form: Student will write a poem about the book or characters using this format.

Tanka: A Tanka is a form of Japanese poetry that depends on the number of lines and syllables instead of rhyme. The pattern is:
Line 1 = 5 syllables, Line 2 = 7 syllables
Line 3 = 5 syllables, Line 4 = 7 syllables
Line 5 = 7 syllables

Example:
  Blue-eyed baby cubs
  wobble out of winter's den
warm sun on cold fur
  forest smells of fresh, cold pine
  wild, new world to grow into.

_____
_____
_____
_____
_____
_____
_____
_____
_____
_____
_____
_____
_____

Newspaper Activity: Student will use this form to write their newspaper piece on then paste it onto their newspaper lay out poster.

Society News Section: Student will write about someone in the story who would be considered a fairly famous person or character. Write a society column about an event or party that they may have attended.

Society News

Creative Writing Activity: Tall Tales:

Tall tales are humorous, exaggerated stories common on the American frontier. Student will write a tall tale about one of the characters in the story and then illustrate it.

Compare and Contrast: Compare and Contrast tell about two or more things and how they are alike or different. Student will write to Compare and Contrast two characters in the story.

_____

- -

_____

_____

- -

_____

_____

- -

_____

_____

- -

_____

_____

- -

_____

_____

- -

_____

_____

- -

_____

_____

- -

_____

Lapbook Activity: Fashion Designer: Student will design clothing that one or more of the characters in the story would have worn. Student will color them or cut them out of scraps of material and put them on the doll form that represents the character and then attach to lapbook.

Poster Board Activity:
Silhouette
Using black construction paper, student will cut out a silhouette of the main character or an item from the story and glue it onto the center of a white or colored 1/2 poster board. Then student will create a frame around the outside with a black poster board.

Creative Art Activity:
Book Mark
Using thick tag board, student will cut into a rectangle 3 inches by 6 inches, and create a book mark that resembles something about the book. Then student will punch a hole in the end and tie ribbon or string through it. Laminate it if possible.

Lesson 8
Activities

Lesson 8 Activities: Students will use the book they are studying and information found on the internet for the following activities. Then the student will write the information required for this activity on the patterns or in their notebook. The patterns may be cut out and placed on the lapbook.

Encyclopedia:
Student will choose one subject from this lesson that interested them and look it up on the internet or in encyclopedia. They will write the name of the subject across the top of the monitor pattern. On the monitor screen section, they will write three or more interesting facts about the subject.

Journal:
Student will imagine that they are one of the characters from the story. After reading each lesson, they will write a short journal entry telling what happened from that character's point of view.
Student will also draw a picture to go along with the journal entry.
At the end of the book, student will staple all the journal entries together to form a complete booklet.
They can even create a special cover for it from construction paper.

Vocabulary word: _____

Definition of the word: _____

_____

_____

Antonym of the word: _____

How many syllables does the word have? _____

Vocabulary Word: _____

Sentence using the word: _____

_____

_____

Synonym of the word: _____

Vocabulary: Student will use the vocabulary words from the list for this lesson. On one of the patterns, or on one index card they will write one vocabulary word. They should also write the definition of the word, then the Antonym and how many Syllables the word has.

On the other card, the student will write the same word. They will write a full sentence using this word and then write the Synonym of the word.

They will repeat this for all the vocabulary words in this lesson.

Place the patterns or cards in an envelope which can be glued into the student's notebook or onto the lapbook..

Sequencing: At the end of the lesson the student will write two of the main events on these two strips. Save them in an envelope which can be glued onto the lapbook or in the notebook. At the end of the book, these strips can be taken out and the student can arrange them in the correct order as they occurred in the story.

_____
_____
_____
_____
_____
_____
_____

Handwriting: Student will pick their favorite sentence that they read in this lesson. Have them write the sentence in their best handwriting on this page or in their notebook.

Student will write out the answers for the following:

Main Idea: In a sentence or two, write what the main idea was of this section.

_____
_____
_____
_____
_____
_____

Key Event: In a sentence or two write what the most important event was in this section.

_____
_____
_____
_____
_____
_____

Prediction: In a sentence of two write what you Predict will happen in the next section.

_____
_____
_____
_____
_____
_____

Comparison: In a sentence of two compare two things in this section. Tell what makes them alike and what makes them different.

_____
_____
_____
_____
_____

Fact or Opinion: In one sentence write a fact about this section and one sentence that is an opinion about the lesson.

_____
_____
_____
_____
_____

Descriptions: Authors use descriptive words so that the reader can imagine the place or thing that is being described. Student will find one place in the book that the author really described well and write the name of the place inside the polygon. On the lines coming out of the polygon, student will write the words the author used to describe the place such as pretty, dark, blue....

Poetry Form: Student will write a poem about the book or characters using this format.

Diamanté: A diamanté is a seven-line, diamond-shaped poem which contrasts two opposites. The pattern is: First Line and seventh line - Name the opposites. Second and sixth lines - Two adjectives describing the opposite nearest it. Third and fifth lines - Three participles (ing words) describing the nearest opposite.
Fourth line - two nouns for each of the opposites.

Example: Fish
silvered, baited
teeming, swimming, darting
scaled amphibian, graceful hind
running, leaping, grazing
hunted, mammal
Deer

Newspaper Activity: Student will use this form to write their newspaper piece on then paste it onto their newspaper lay out poster.

Sports Section: Student will imagine that one of the characters in your book is in a sports competition and write a newspaper article about it and then illustrate it as well.

Sports

Creative Writing Activity: Memoir: When writing a memoir, a person chooses one time or one event and expounds upon it by stretching the truth. Student will write a memoir as if they were a character in the story. They should choose one event to write about, and stretch the truth in the retelling.

My Memoir

_____
_____
_____
_____
_____
_____
_____
_____
_____
_____
_____
_____
_____
_____
_____
_____
_____
_____
_____
_____
_____
_____
_____
_____
_____
_____
_____
_____
_____
_____
_____
_____
_____
_____
_____

Writing Skills Activity: Student will use this form or write in their notebook.

Sequel: A sequel is a movie or book that follows another. The sequel contains the same characters and follows the same story line. The characters and story line may change during the sequel but they have to start out the same to show the connection with the previous story. Students will write the first few paragraphs of a sequel for this story.

_____

- -

_____

_____

- -

_____

_____

- -

_____

_____

- -

_____

_____

- -

_____

_____

- -

_____

_____

- -

_____

_____

- -

_____

Writing Skills Activity: Student will use this form or write in their notebook.

Lapbook Activity: Book Cover Puzzle:
Student will glue a picture they print from the internet of the book cover, onto this puzzle pattern so that the pattern shows on the back. Then student will cut the book cover into puzzle pieces. This can go in an envelope on the lapbook to be put together later.

Poster Board Activity:
Board Game
Student will create a board game on the poster board to use with this story.

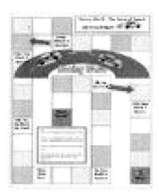

Creative Art Activity:
Photography
Photography is a great form of art. Student will find things that reminds them of this book and take some photos of it. Get these printed in black and white and some in color.
Student can turn these into cards, frame them or take photos of one item in different angles and create a unique photo like this one.

Lesson 9
Activity

Lesson 9 Activities: Students will use the book they are studying and information found on the internet for the following activities. Then the student will write the information required for this activity on the patterns or in their notebook. The patterns may be cut out and placed on the lapbook.

Encyclopedia:
Student will choose one subject from this lesson that interested them and look it up on the internet or in encyclopedia. They will write the name of the subject across the top of the monitor pattern. On the monitor screen section, they will write three or more interesting facts about the subject.

Journal:
Student will imagine that they are one of the characters from the story. After reading each lesson, they will write a short journal entry telling what happened from that character's point of view.
Student will also draw a picture to go along with the journal entry.
At the end of the book, student will staple all the journal entries together to form a complete booklet.
They can even create a special cover for it from construction paper.

Vocabulary word: _____

Definition of the word: _____

_____

_____

Antonym of the word: _____

How many syllables does the word have? _____

Vocabulary Word: _____

Sentence using the word: _____

_____

_____

Synonym of the word: _____

Vocabulary: Student will use the vocabulary words from the list for this lesson. On one of the patterns, or on one index card they will write one vocabulary word. They should also write the definition of the word, then the Antonym and how many Syllables the word has.

On the other card, the student will write the same word. They will write a full sentence using this word and then write the Synonym of the word.

They will repeat this for all the vocabulary words in this lesson.

Place the patterns or cards in an envelope which can be glued into the student's notebook or onto the lapbook..

Sequencing: At the end of the lesson the student will write two of the main events on these two strips. Save them in an envelope which can be glued onto the lapbook or in the notebook. At the end of the book, these strips can be taken out and the student can arrange them in the correct order as they occurred in the story.

Handwriting: Student will pick their favorite sentence that they read in this lesson. Have them write the sentence in their best handwriting on this page or in their notebook.

Student will write out the answers for the following:

Main Idea: In a sentence or two, write what the main idea was of this section.

_____
_____
_____
_____
_____

Key Event: In a sentence or two write what the most important event was in this section.

_____
_____
_____
_____
_____

Prediction: In a sentence of two write what you Predict will happen in the next section.

_____
_____
_____
_____
_____

Comparison: In a sentence of two compare two things in this section. Tell what makes them alike and what makes them different.

_____
_____
_____
_____
_____

Fact or Opinion: In one sentence write a fact about this section and one sentence that is an opinion about the lesson.

_____
_____
_____
_____
_____

Pyramid of Importance: Each character in the story holds a position of importance. Some are of main importance, some are of less importance. Student will fill in the pyramid with the names of the characters. The top should have the most important character, the next line the next most important characters and continue down until you have listed all the characters in order of importance.

Poetry Form: Student will write a poem about the book or characters using this format.

Lantern: A lantern is a five line poem in the shape of a Japanese lantern. The Pattern is:

Line 1: noun (one syllable)
Line 2: describe the noun (two syllables)
Line 3: describe the noun (three syllables
Line 4: describe the noun (four syllables)
Line 5: Synonym for noun in line one (one syllable)

Example:	Mane
	long, thick
	blonde to black
	royal mantle
	Fur

Newspaper Activity: Student will use this form to write their newspaper piece on then paste it onto their newspaper lay out poster.

Entertainment Section: Book Review Student will write an over all review of the book and tell what they liked and did not like, which characters seemed real and which scenes were described the best. Student should also ad a picture of the book cover.

Book Review

Creative Writing Activity: Newberry Award: Each year one book is chosen to receive the John Newberry Award for great writing. Student will write a short report on why this book did or should have won the award.

_____

_____

_____

_____

_____

_____

_____

_____

_____

_____

_____

_____

_____

_____

_____

_____

_____

_____

_____

_____

_____

_____

_____

_____

_____

_____

_____

_____

_____

_____

_____

_____

_____

Writing Skills Activity: Student will use this form or write in their notebook.

Climax: The climax of a story is the point where the reader knows who wins the conflict or how the problem will be solved. Student will write what the main problem was and at what point they knew how it would be solved.

_____

- -

_____

_____

- -

_____

_____

- -

_____

_____

- -

_____

_____

- -

_____

_____

- -

_____

_____

- -

_____

_____

- -

_____

Lapbook Activity: Mini Book: Student will make a mini book about this story or about a subject in the story. See the pattern on one of the following pages.

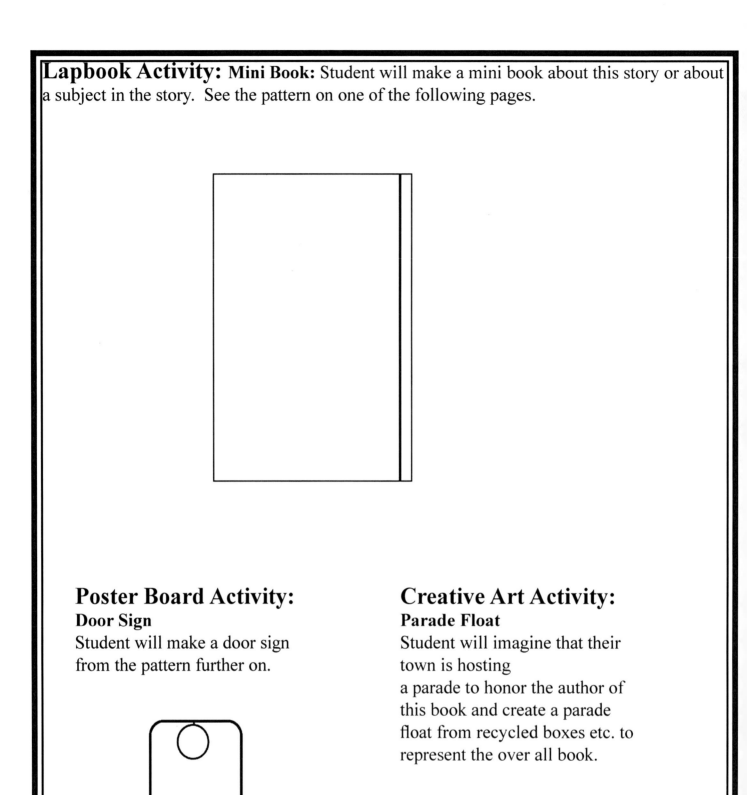

Poster Board Activity:
Door Sign
Student will make a door sign from the pattern further on.

Creative Art Activity:
Parade Float
Student will imagine that their town is hosting a parade to honor the author of this book and create a parade float from recycled boxes etc. to represent the over all book.

Door Sign: On a piece of poster board student will create a sign for their bedroom door that represents something from the book.

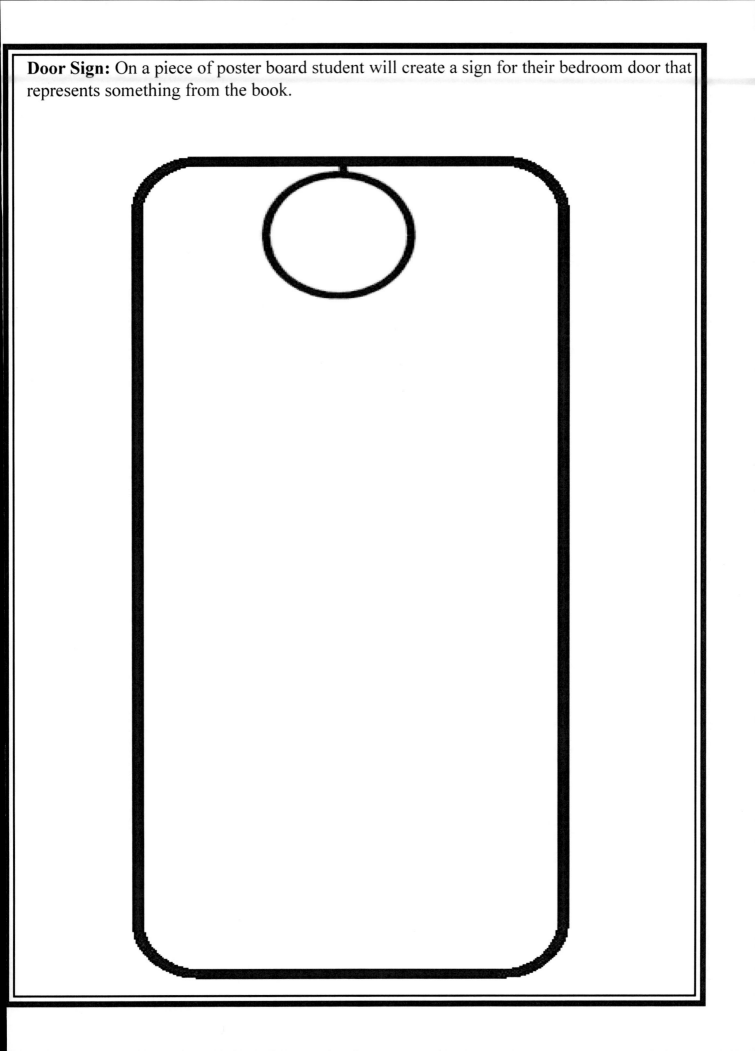

Mini Book : Student will create a mini book that retells the story. This may be put on the Lapbook.

12

1

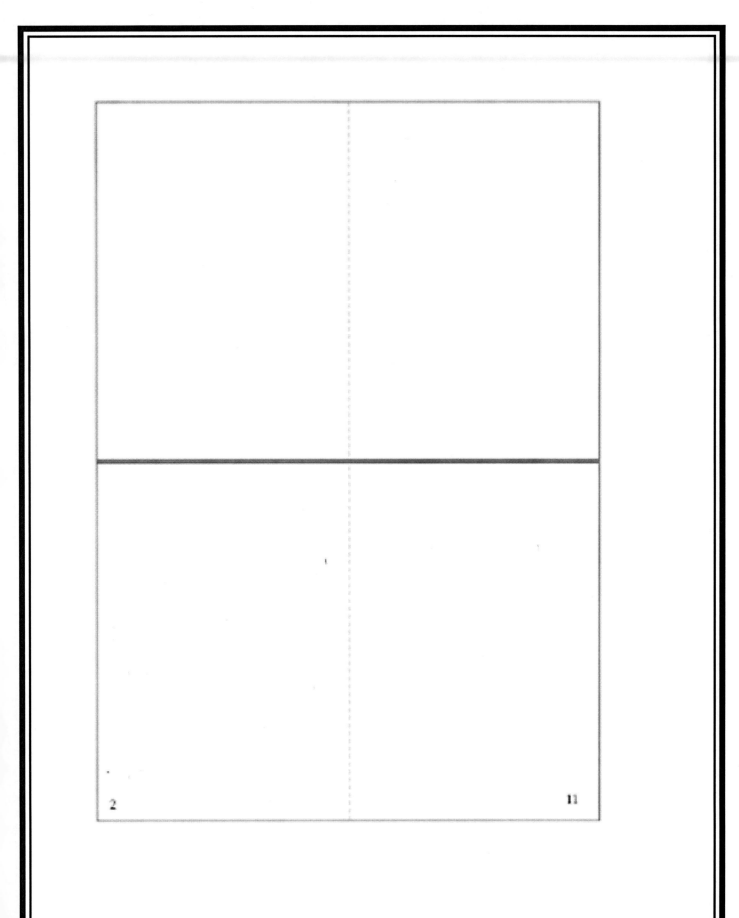

2   11

10

3

8

5

4

9

6

7

Lesson 10
Activities

Lesson 10 Activities: Students will use the book they are studying and information found on the internet for the following activities. Then the student will write the information required for this activity on the patterns or in their notebook. The patterns may be cut out and placed on the lapbook.

Encyclopedia:
Student will choose one subject from this lesson that interested them and look it up on the internet or in encyclopedia. They will write the name of the subject across the top of the monitor pattern. On the monitor screen section, they will write three or more interesting facts about the subject.

Journal:
Student will imagine that they are one of the characters from the story. After reading each lesson, they will write a short journal entry telling what happened from that character's point of view.
Student will also draw a picture to go along with the journal entry.
At the end of the book, student will staple all the journal entries together to form a complete booklet.
They can even create a special cover for it from construction paper.

Vocabulary word: _____
Definition of the word: _____
_____
_____

Antonym of the word: _____
How many syllables does the word have? _____

Vocabulary Word: _____
Sentence using the word: _____
_____
_____

Synonym of the word: _____

Vocabulary: Student will use the vocabulary words from the list for this lesson. On one of the patterns, or on one index card they will write one vocabulary word. They should also write the definition of the word, then the Antonym and how many Syllables the word has.

On the other card, the student will write the same word. They will write a full sentence using this word and then write the Synonym of the word.

They will repeat this for all the vocabulary words in this lesson.

Place the patterns or cards in an envelope which can be glued into the student's notebook or onto the lapbook..

Sequencing: At the end of the lesson the student will write two of the main events on these two strips. Save them in an envelope which can be glued onto the lapbook or in the notebook. At the end of the book, these strips can be taken out and the student can arrange them in the correct order as they occurred in the story.

_____
_____
_____
_____
_____
_____
_____

Handwriting: Student will pick their favorite sentence that they read in this lesson. Have them write the sentence in their best handwriting on this page or in their notebook.

Student will write out the answers for the following:

Main Idea: In a sentence or two, write what the main idea was of this section.

_____
_____
_____
_____
_____
_____

Key Event: In a sentence or two write what the most important event was in this section.

_____
_____
_____
_____
_____
_____

Prediction: In a sentence of two write what you Predict will happen in the next section.

_____
_____
_____
_____
_____
_____

Comparison: In a sentence of two compare two things in this section. Tell what makes them alike and what makes them different.

_____
_____
_____
_____
_____

Fact or Opinion: In one sentence write a fact about this section and one sentence that is an opinion about the lesson.

_____
_____
_____
_____
_____

Hero vs. Villain: Most stories usually have a hero (the main character) and a villain. The villain may not seem that bad. The villain is usually the character who stands in the way of the main character, or against the main character. Student will name the Hero and the Villain and fill in the "What the Villain does...." square.

What the Villain does to hinder the Hero.

Hero

Villain

Poetry Form: Student will write a poem about the book or characters using this format.

Shape Poem: To be done on a separate sheet of paper. Shape poems can be made by placing words, which describe a particular object, in such a way that they form the shape of the object. Student will start by making a simple outline of the shape or object (an animal, a football, a fruit etc.) large enough to fill a piece of paper. Then student will brainstorm a minimum of ten words and phrases that describe the shape including action and feeling words as well. Next, student will place a piece of paper over the shape and decide where the words are going to be placed so that they outline the shape but also fit well together. Separate words and phrases with commas. Shape poems can also be created by simply filling in the shape with a poem, as well.

Newspaper Activity: Student will use this form to write their newspaper piece on then paste it onto their newspaper lay out poster.

Word Search Section: Find all the words

```
Y  L  T  N  E  L  O  V  E  L  A  M  P  S  J
V  T  O  F  D  E  M  R  I  F  N  O  C  R  M
E  U  I  P  O  E  M  P  H  A  T  I  C  E  E
D  V  L  L  P  R  C  H  E  A  T  I  N  G  T
I  E  I  N  I  O  M  L  F  E  B  H  N  G  I
C  X  D  S  E  B  R  I  H  X  D  I  A  A  C
I  P  E  L  N  R  I  T  D  D  D  M  L  B  U
T  O  S  B  X  E  A  S  U  A  E  A  T  L  L
C  U  O  J  L  P  H  B  N  N  B  V  U  E  O
E  N  L  P  M  A  I  E  I  O  I  L  Q  P  U
S  D  C  Y  L  O  M  T  R  L  P  T  E  R  S
N  I  S  Q  U  O  I  E  J  P  I  S  Y  A  L
I  N  I  S  R  E  Y  X  S  J  P  T  E  C  Y
U  G  D  P  S  E  L  B  I  D  U  A  Y  R  B
L  E  T  H  A  R  G  I  C  A  L  L  Y  K  C
```

AMENITIES	APPREHENSIVE
AUDIBLE	BLAMES
CARPETBAGGERS	CHEATING
CONFIRMED	DISCLOSED
DUBIOUS	EMPHATIC
EQUAL	EXPOUNDING
FORMIDABLE	INSECTICIDE
LETHARGICALLY	MALEVOLENTLY
METICULOUSLY	OPPORTUNITY
PLOY	PROMENADING
RESPONSIBILITY	UNSYMPATHETIC
VULNERABILITY	

Creative Writing Activity: A Different End: Student will write a different ending for the story.

_____
_____
_____
_____
_____
_____
_____
_____
_____
_____
_____
_____
_____
_____
_____
_____
_____
_____
_____
_____
_____
_____
_____
_____
_____
_____
_____
_____

Writing Skills Activity: Plot Analysis Board

Student will create this by following the directions.

What you need:
Index Cards, Pictures from the internet, Markers, Crayons. Glue

1. Fold the poster board in half so that it makes a folder.
2. Decorate the front of the folder with pictures and information that includes the Title, the Author, the Illustrator, and the Publisher.
3. On index cards, write the information requested below. Glue the index cards inside the folder. You can put pictures on the cards to go along with them.

   Information to put on cards:
   1. Main Character and Character Traits
   2. Main Setting
   3. Other Characters
   4. Other Settings in the Story
   5. Main Problem
   6. Other Problems
   7. Climax
   8. Solution to the Problem
   9. Your favorite part of the story
   10. What you would change if you could about the story.

Lapbook Activity: The Commandments:

Student will cut out the patter and fold so that the Ten Commandments are on the front. Inside student will write how a character may have broken or upheld one or more of these commandments. Attach to Lapbook.

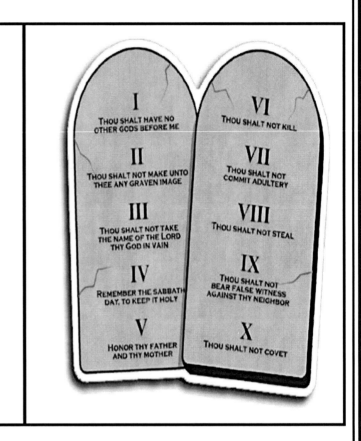

Poster Board Activity:
Jeopardy

On the poster board student will create a game board like the one on the next page. They will cut out several sets of the play money. The teacher will write 4 to 8 questions for each category. The student then picks one category and the dollar amount of the question they will try and answer. The teacher or student reads the question. If the answer is correct the student wins the amount of money that they chose. The next player takes a turn. The winner is the one with the most

Creative Art Activity:
Sketch

Student will imagine they are a sketch artist and using black pencils or charcoal pencils, they will sketch some of the main characters, places or events from the story.

JEOPARDY

People	Places	Animals	Other
$100	$100	$100	$100
$200	$200	$200	$200
$300	$300	$300	$300
$400	$400	$400	$400

Additional
Activities

Additional Writing Activities

Imaginative: Imaginative writing is when you write a fanciful story using your imagination. Student will write one that comes to mind while they read this book.

Essay: An essay is a short piece of writing, from an author's personal point of view. Student will write a short essay from their point of view about a subject that comes to mind while reading these books.

Speech: A speech is the act of delivering a formal spoken communication to an audience . Student will write a short speech that one of the characters from the books may have given.

Autobiography: An autobiography is a story of a person's life. Student will write a short autobiography outline of one of the characters or they could write about the author as well.

Humor: Humor allows the reader to laugh and enjoy a story. Student will write a humorous piece about a subject or thing mentioned in these books.

ABC Story: ABC Stories are short stories that have each sentence starting with the next letter in the alphabet. Student will write a short ABC story about an event or one of the characters in the book. For example:
 A girl named Kit lived in America. By noon she was happy...

Literature Web: A story will make you think of many things and feel many things. Student will draw this chart in their notebook and fill it in.

Key Words: What were some important words or phrases?

Feelings: What feelings did you have while reading the book?

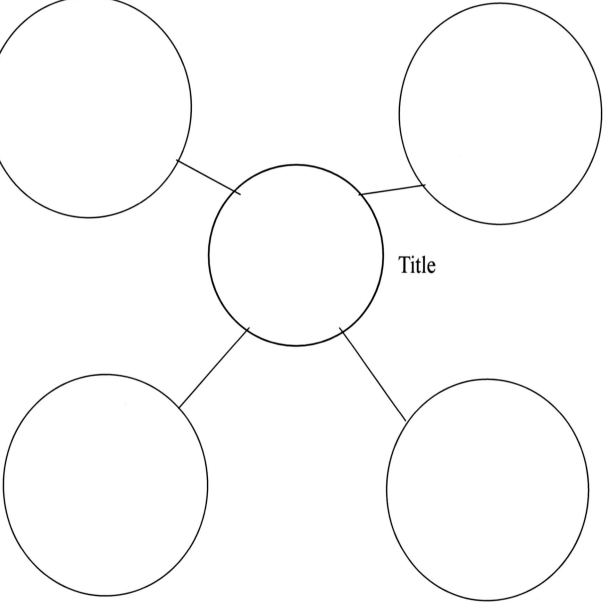

Title

Symbols: Did the author use any symbols in the story?

Attitude: What do you think the authors attitude is about the subject this story is about?

Sign Language:

On a piece of poster board, student will glue a larger versions of the sign language alphabet. Now the teacher will sign a name, scene or vocabulary word from the story. Students try to figure the word out by pointing to the correct sign language letter and spelling out the words.

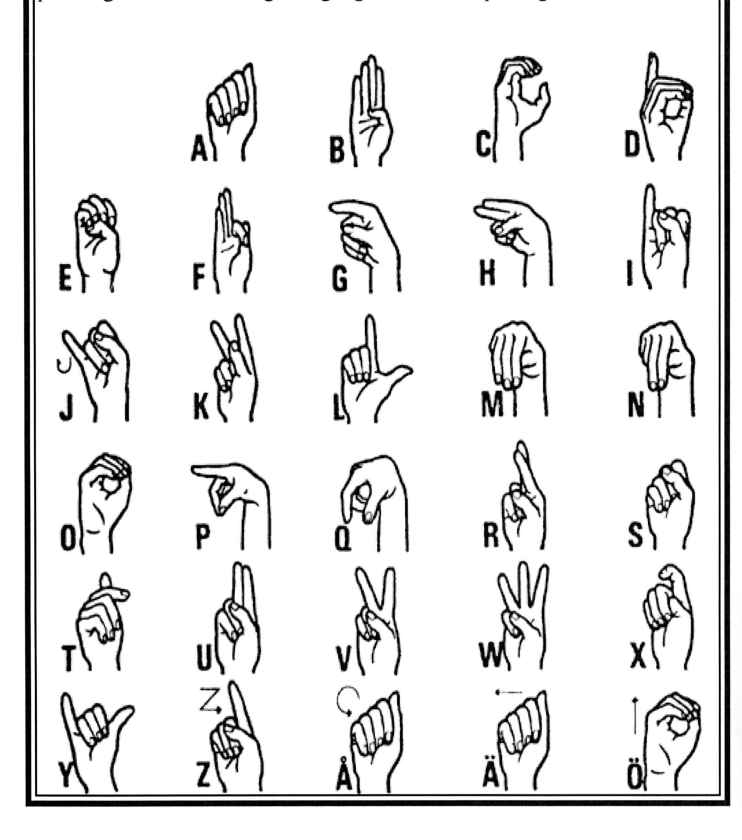

Theater Box:

Get a cardboard box with a flat side larger than a piece of paper. In the side cut out a square about 6 by 9 inches. This will be the opening for your theater.

While reading each chapter of the book, Student will draw one or more of the main scenes on 8 1/2 by 11 inch drawing paper. Stay within the inner 6 by 9 inches though. Color these with markers, paint, colored pencils etc.

Figure out a way that these pictures can be slid in and out of the box, so they appear in the opening and it looks like you are changing scenes, or draw them all on one long roll, and create rollers in each end of the box out of paper towel rolls.

At the end of the book you should have a whole story in these scenes. Present the scenes in your theater to family or friends. You will have to act as the announcer and explain the main events in each scene.

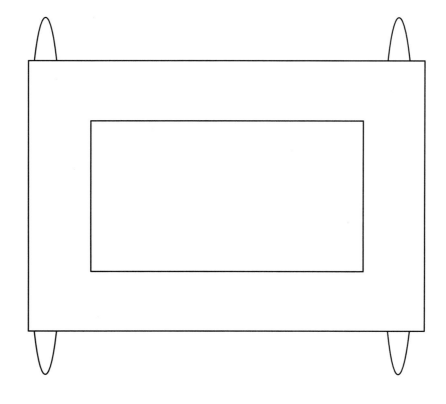

Acting: Student will

1. Dress up as one of the characters in the story. They can act out their favorite part of the story.
2. Host a talk show where another member of the family acts as the television host. Your student is the main character of the story. They ask you questions about the story.
3. Hold a trial. Someone dresses up as the villain in the story. Someone dresses up as the main character. Someone as a lawyer and someone as a judge. Hold a trial to determine if the villain is really guilty of crimes or not.

Rock Art:
Student will gather smooth rocks of different shapes and sizes. Student will clean the rocks and when dry create characters from the book with the rocks, by painting them, making clothes for them and gluing on google eyes.

Name Art:
Student will write the main characters name in the middle of 1/4 poster board and then decorate all around it in any art form they like.

Carving:

Use soap or wax and carve a character from the story. All you need to carve soap is a bar of soap and a spoon. If your child is old enough to use a butter knife then you can let them have a butter knife to carve their soap with. Soap carving can be messy so it is best to be done on a table covered with an old cloth or newspaper. And everyone doing the carving should have old clothes on.

When carving soap, you can use any size bar of soap you would like, but a nice big bar of soap is better to get creative with. If you are lucky enough to have a bar of home made lye soap that will work as well. Unwrap your bar of soap and decide what you want to make with your bar of soap. Soap is a soft material so a spoon will work to carve a bar of soap just fine. A knife can give your bar of soap more detail then a spoon can but it is more dangerous.

Sewing:

Use felt and material stuffing. Create a pattern for something from the story such as an animal or character. Cut out two of the same patterns from the felt. Have student sew around the outside edges. Stuff with stuffing and complete the sewing.

Design a Needlepoint:
Get graph paper and have student design a needlepoint by placing an x in the boxes to design the picture.

Shape Puzzle: On poster board student will draw out a large copy of the shape of a character or item from the book. Cut it into a puzzle pattern.

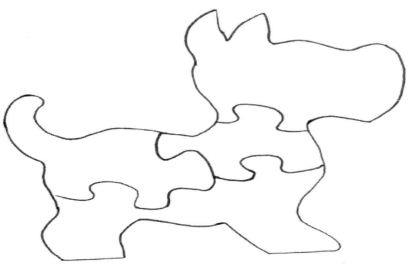

I Spy

Student will find pictures on the internet of things that come to mind while reading this book. Pictures of the characters, of the vocabulary words etc. Student will print and then glue them all over the poster board. Now they should make an I spy set of calling cards on index cards.

For example your cards would say:

I spy a cat.

I spy a rat.

Give the cards to a younger child and see if they can find all the items on the I spy poster.

Bingo: Print as many of these Bingo boards as you need for the students. Write the vocabulary words in the squares of the Bingo boards. Each board should be different. Use the definition index cards as the call cards for the game.

B	I	N	G	O
		Free Space		

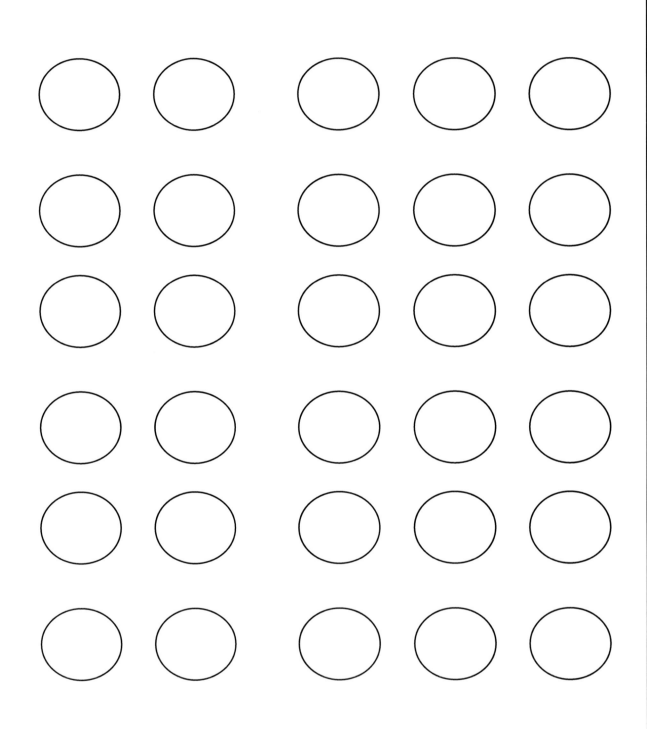

Comprehension

The following pages have the
Fill in the Blanks,
True and False,
Multiple Choice
and
Who, What, Where, When,
Why and How Questions
for all lessons.

Use the Vocabulary words
on the following page for the
questions

Lesson 1   Chapter 1,2
Lesson 2   Chapter 3
Lesson 3   Chapter 4
Lesson 4   Chapter 5
Lesson 5   Chapter 6
Lesson 6   Chapter 7
Lesson 7   Chapter 8
Lesson 8   Chapter 9
Lesson 9   Chapter 10
Lesson 10   Chapter 11,12

Vocabulary Words:
Lesson 1. meticulously disposition mortgage dubious monotonous temerity bale formidable chiffonier maverick

Lesson 2. resiliency humiliation embittered ignorant outwit moronic conspiratorially oblivious careened maneuvered

Lesson 3. confirmed expounding feigned trust objections cheating faltered emphatic   ploy disclosed

Lesson 4. prevailed obnoxious personality regular promenading humiliated sullenly solemnly malevolently insult

Lesson 5. dumbfounded confounded bewildered obedience profitable equal respect indignant opportunity herbs

Lesson 6. permanently flounce apprehensive interminable superior collateral mulatto goaded boycott carpetbaggers

Lesson 7. suspiciously prideful forgiving sensibly seriousness pondered threatened prophesied confided gossip

Lesson 8. enveloped persnickety indefinitely audible resigned amenities despairingly unsympathetic skittish confident

Lesson 9. borrow ginned insecticide blames digesting urgency shroud lethargically scheme suffocating

Lesson 10. compassion intended responsibility vulnerability crescendo trigger kerosene transfixed adamant identify

Fill in the Blanks: Write the vocabulary word that best completes the sentence.
Words: mortgage   monotonous   meticulously   formidable   chiffonier

1. Always _____ neat, Little Man never allowed dirt, tears, or stains to mar anything he owned.
2. There is a _____ on two hundred acres of the Logan land.
3. Suddenly, Cassie grew conscious of a break in that _____ tone and looked up.
4. Gazing at the most _____ being they had ever seen, the children huddled closer to father.
5. Mama has a grand _____ with a floor length mirror in her bedroom.

True / False: Write T if statement is true; write F if it is false.
1. _____ Stacey, Christopher-John, and Little Man are Cassie's three brothers.
2. _____ It was Cassie's Grandpa who bought the land in 1887 and added more in 1918.
3. _____ T.J. And Claude Avery are cousins of the Logan family.
4. _____ Cassie and Little Man do not like T.J.

Multiple Choice: Write ABCD in the space for the best answer.
1. _____ How many acres does the Logan family own?
A. 20
B. 400
C. 50
D. 100

2. _____ Who is in the class that Cassie's mother is teaching?
A. Stacey
B. T.J.
C. both A and B
D. none of the Logan children

3. _____ What school do the white children go to?
A. Jefferson Davis County School
B. Confederacy County School
C. Mississippi County School
D. Robert E. Lee County School

4. _____ The black children go to the _____ School.
A. Lincoln County Black
B. Federal Union County
C. Mississippi Black Children Elementary
D. Great Faith Elementary and Secondary

Lesson 1
Write full sentences for this section:

1. Who is Clayton Chester Logan?
2. What made the black children angry over the books?
3. Where did the burnings of the Berry family take place?
4. When does school start and end at the Great Faith School?
5. Why does Cassie's father have to work away from the farm?
6. How long has Mary Logan been a teacher at the Great Faith School?

(Who) _____
_____
_____
_____

(What)_____
_____
_____
_____

(Where)_____
_____
_____
_____

(When)_____
_____
_____
_____

(Why)_____
_____
_____
_____

(How)_____
_____
_____
_____

Lesson 2   Chapter 3

Fill in the Blanks: Write the vocabulary word that best completes the sentence.
Words: maneuvered   ignorant   humiliation   outwit   oblivious

1. No one was more angered by this _____ than Little Man.
2. Big Ma told the children to pay no mind to the _____ white folks.
3. It was as if the bus were a living thing, plaguing the children at every turn, they could not _____ it.
4. For once Little Man was happily _____ to the mud spattering upon him.
5. "Oh, how sweet was well _____ revenge," thought Cassie.

True / False: Write T if statement is true; write F if it is false.
1. _____ The children didn't have to go to school because of the heavy rain.
2. _____ The Jefferson Davis school bus driver liked to entertain his passengers.
3. _____ The Great Faith School has one small bus for its students to ride.
4. _____ T.J. and Stacey made a trap for the Jefferson Davis School bus.

Multiple Choice: Write ABCD in the space for the best answer.
1. _____ What white boy never rides the bus no matter how bad the weather is?
A. Bill Jones
B. Tom Mc Cain
C. Jeremy Simms
D. Jefferson Davis Halley

2. _____ Jason is the Logan family's _____.
A. dog
B. horse
C. mule
D. cow

3._____ What was Big Ma looking for under the bed?
A. a blanket
B. a rifle
C. a club
D. a pair of slippers

4. _____ The white bus driver's name is _____.
A. John Granville
B. Jefferson Lee
C. George Davis
D. Ted Grimes

Lesson 2
Write full sentences for this section:

1. Who made the trap for the white school bus?
2. What happened to the bus when it fell in the ditch?
3. Where will the school have to send the bus to get it repaired?
4. When will the bus be fixed?
5. Why does the white boy Jeremy Simms hang around the black boys?
6. How did the Logans find out about the night riders?

(Who) _____
_____
_____
_____

(What)_____
_____
_____
_____

(Where)_____
_____
_____
_____

(When)_____
_____
_____
_____

(Why)_____
_____
_____
_____

(How)_____
_____
_____
_____

Lesson 3   Chapter 4

Fill in the Blanks: Write the vocabulary word that best completes the sentence.
Words: trust   objections   cheating   confirmed   faltered

1. If Cassie lets tears fall, her mother's suspicion that something is wrong will be _____.
2. T.J. is not a person anyone can _____, he can never make a true friend.
3. The Logan children took to Mr. Morrison and had no _____ to cleaning the old shack.
4. T.J. is planning on _____ on his history test.
5. Cassie _____ for a moment before deciding that her bottom was more important than Stacey's code of honor.

True / False: Write T if statement is true; write F if it is false.
1. _____ All the Logan children have been so quiet that their mama and Big Ma are worried.
2. _____ Stacey thought it was a good idea for everyone to have some fun at Wallace's Store.
3. _____ Stacey really liked Mr. Morrison from the first day he came.
4. _____ Mr. Morrison is going to tell Stacey's mama that he was at the Wallace's store.

Multiple Choice: Write ABCD in the space for the best answer.
1. _____ Mr. Morrison is a _____.
A. quiet man
B. shy person
C. private person
D. all the above

2. _____ Who stopped the fight between Stacey and T.J.?
A. Mr. Morrison
B. the sheriff
C. the night riders
D. Stacey's mama

3._____ After the Civil War, who bought two thousand acres from Fillmore Granger?
A. an Indian tribe
B. a Yankee Mr. Hollenbeck
C. Cassie's Grandpa
D. the Union Army

4. _____ Who set fire to Mr. Berry and his nephews?
A. the Grangers
B. the Jacksons
C. The Wallaces
D. the Davis clan

Lesson 3
Write full sentences for this section:

1. Who were the night riders looking for?
2. What did Mr. Granger want from Big Ma?
3. Where does Mrs. Logan do her shopping?
4. When Stacey and T.J. were taking the history test, what happened?
5. Why did the night riders tar and feather poor Mr. Tatum?
6. How did Paul Edward make a living after his mama died?

(Who) _____
_____
_____
_____

(What)_____
_____
_____
_____

(Where)_____
_____
_____
_____

(When)_____
_____
_____
_____

(Why)_____
_____
_____
_____

(How)_____
_____
_____
_____

Lesson 4   Chapter 5

Fill in the Blanks: Write the vocabulary word that best completes the sentence.
Words: prevailed   insult   regular   humiliated   sullenly

1. When Big Ma _____, Jack finally settled into a moderate trot.
2. Big Ma has some _____ customers who buy her milk and eggs at the market.
3. Cassie was so _____ she screamed with anger towards Mr. Barnett.
4. A second _____ in one day was too much for Cassie to bear.
5. Stacey _____ crossed the street, putting his hands in his pockets.

True / False: Write T if statement is true; write F if it is false.
1. _____ Strawberry, Mississippi is a large modern city with many stores and businesses.
2. _____ Big Ma parks her wagon at the back of the market because the white folks wagons are at the front.
3. _____ The Logan children like Mr. Jamison, he reminded them of their papa.
4. _____ Barnett Mercantile had everything, even handguns.

Multiple Choice: Write ABCD in the space for the best answer.
1. _____ What event takes place every second Saturday of the month in Strawberry?
A. a dance
B. market day
C. a concert
D. a sing along

2. _____ Wade W. Jamison is an _____.
A. attorney-at-law
B. a doctor
C. a postal clerk
D. a dentist

3._____ Who went to Strawberry with Big Ma?
A. T.J.
B. Cassie
C. Stacey
D. all the above

4. _____ Lillian Jean is Jeremy's _____.
A. cousin
B. mother
C. sister
D. aunt

Lesson 4
Write full sentences for this section:

1. Who tried to help Cassie when Lillian Jean's father attacked her?
2. What did T.J. show Stacey at the store?
3. Where was Big Ma when Cassie, Stacey, and T.J. went to the store?
4. When Cassie accidentally bumped into Lillian Jean, what happened?
5. Why did Mr. Barnett leave T.J.'s order to help other people?
6. How did Cassie feel about her first day in Strawberry?

(Who) _____
_____
_____
_____

(What)_____
_____
_____
_____

(Where)_____
_____
_____
_____

(When)_____
_____
_____
_____

(Why)_____
_____
_____
_____

(How)_____
_____
_____
_____

Fill in the Blanks: Write the vocabulary word that best completes the sentence.
Words: dumbfounded   respect   bewildered   opportunity   profitable

1. Throwing open the door of Mama's room, Stacey and Cassie stood _____ in the doorway.
2. Christopher-John looked somewhat _____ by all that has happened.
3. The white people who sold slaves thought it was a very _____ venture.
4. What _____ the black people give their own people is far more important, because it's given freely.
5. "The _____, dear sister, was too much to resist," laughed Uncle Hammer.

True / False: Write T if statement is true; write F if it is false.
1. _____ Cassie was afraid to tell Uncle Hammer what happened in Strawberry.
2. _____ Cassie's mama did not know what happened in Strawberry.
3. _____ Teaching Christianity to slaves didn't make them stop wanting to be free.
4. _____ Slavery was not a very profitable business before the Civil war started.

Multiple Choice: Write ABCD in the space for the best answer.
1. _____ What did Stacey find in the barn?
A. an old horse
B. a new milk cow
C. a silver Packard
D. an old pick-up truck

2. _____ Who did the Packard belong to?
A. Uncle Hammer
B. Mr. Jamison
C. Mrs. Simms
D. Mr. Granger

3. _____ Where did Big Ma learn medicine?
A. from an Indian medicine man
B. Papa Luke
C. from a university
D. helping in a doctor's office

4. _____ Who is Papa Luke?
A. a school teacher
B. a carpenter
C. a university professor
D. Cassie's great-grandpa

Lesson 5
Write full sentences for this section:

1. Who comes every winter to spend Christmas with the Logans?
2. What knowledge did Papa Luke have?
3. Where did the Logans bump into the Wallaces as they drove home from church?
4. When a black person gives respect to another black person, what kind of respect is it?
5. Why do the white people demand respect from the black people?
6. How did some people feel about the black people after the Civil war was over?

(Who) _____
_____
_____
_____

(What) _____
_____
_____
_____

(Where) _____
_____
_____
_____

(When) _____
_____
_____
_____

(Why) _____
_____
_____
_____

(How) _____
_____
_____

Fill in the Blanks: Write the vocabulary word that best completes the sentence.
Words: flounce   permanently   boycott   apprehensive   goaded

1. As far as Uncle Hammer was concerned, T.J. could keep the coat _____.
2. Christopher-John, Little Man, and Cassie exchanged _____ glances.
3. Lillian Jean managed to _____ past Cassie with a superior smirk twice that week.
4. Cassie watched her brother to see if he was going to let himself be _____ by T.J.
5. The Logans are pointing a finger at the Wallaces with their idea to _____ their store.

True / False: Write T if statement is true; write F if it is false.
1. _____ Stacey gave his new coat to T.J.
2. _____ Uncle Hammer gave Stacey a whipping because he gave his coat away.
3. _____ Papa never did make it home for Christmas this year.
4. _____ All of the Logans are natural born fast runners.

Multiple Choice: Write ABCD in the space for the best answer.
1. _____ That Christmas Eve, what did the Logan family share?
A. old Christmas tales
B. cookies and punch
C. old memories
D. old gossip

2. _____ How old was Mr. Morrison when his parents died?
A. 6 years
B. 1 year
C. 10 years
D. 3 years

3. _____ The French author Alexander Dumas is a _____.
A. woman
B. white man
C. American Indian
D. a black man

4. _____ What did each Logan child receive for Christmas?
A. toys
B. books
C. boots
D. hats

Lesson 6
Write full sentences for this section:

1. Who were killed by the night riders many years ago?
2. What principle did Stacy learn from Uncle Hammer?
3. Where are Papa, Uncle Hammer, and Mr. Morrison getting supplies?
4. When everyone left church on Christmas, who did the Logans invite to dinner?
5. Why did Stacey give T.J. his new coat?
6. How did everyone get a shock and surprise on Christmas day?

(Who) _____

_____

_____

_____

(What)_____

_____

_____

_____

(Where)_____

_____

_____

_____

(When)_____

_____

_____

_____

(Why)_____

_____

_____

_____

(How)_____

_____

_____

_____

Fill in the Blanks: Write the vocabulary word that best completes the sentence.
Words: gossip forgiving sensibly threatened prideful

1. "Mama gonna whip you good," said _____ Little Man to his sister.
2. _____ is not letting something nag at you rotting you out.
3. A person has to clear their head before he can think _____.
4. All Cassie had to do to prime the _____ pump was smile nicely and whisper.
5. Lillian Jean _____ to tell her father about the fight.

True / False: Write T if statement is true; write F if it is false.
1. _____ Papa told Cassie she should do what Lillian Jean tells her to because she's white.
2. _____ If Cassie makes a wrong decision and Mr. Simms gets involved, then Papa will have to get involved.
3. _____ All the month of January Cassie walked with Lillian Jean.
4. _____ Cassie and Lillian Jean had a fist fight.

Multiple Choice: Write ABCD in the space for the best answer.
1. _____ When Cassie was walking with Lillian Jean what did she do?
A. share her leftover lunch
B. carry Lillian Jean's books
C. carry Lillian Jean's lunch bag
D. carry Lillian Jean's coat

2. _____ Where did Papa tell Cassie she got her temper from?
A. Paul Edward
B. Grandma
C. himself
D. Uncle Hammer

3. _____ When Cassie and Lillian Jean are alone what does Lillian do?
A. gives her old clothes to Cassie
B. gives her little gifts
C. she tells Cassie her secrets
D. invites Cassie to dinner

4. _____ Who came to the school and fired Mrs. Logan?
A. Mr. Granger
B. Mr. Wallace
C. Mr. Jamison
D. Mr. Jones

Lesson 7
Write full sentences for this section:

1. Who was caught cheating again on the school exams?
2. What did Cassie threaten Lillian Jean with after the fight?
3. Where did T.J. go to make trouble for Mrs. Logan?
4. When T.J. said he had to figure something out to pass the final exams what did Stacey tell him to do?
5. Why would anyone at Jefferson Davis school laugh at Lillian Jean for loosing the fight?
6. How does a person gain respect?

(Who) _____
_____
_____
_____

(What)_____
_____
_____
_____

(Where)_____
_____
_____
_____

(When)_____
_____
_____
_____

(Why)_____
_____
_____
_____

(How)_____
_____
_____

Fill in the Blanks: Write the vocabulary word that best completes the sentence.
Words: despairingly   enveloped   unsympathetic   audible   confident

1. Rain drenched the air with fresh, vital life, as spring _____ all around all of us.
2. "What did Mr. Jamison want?" Mama asked, her voice barely _____.
3. It was clear my mama is _____ to Mr. Avery's problem.
4. Stacey sighed _____ and sat down to explain what happened to T.J.
5. "Mama's too busy," Cassie said, folding her arms and feeling _____ Stacy would tell her the whole story.

True / False: Write T if statement is true; write F if it is false.
1. _____ T.J. is hanging out with Jeremy's two older brothers, R.W. and Melvin.
2. _____ T.J.'s parents are not able to control T.J.'s actions any longer.
3. _____ Papa and Mr. Morrison left Stacey home the day they went to Vicksburg.
4. _____ Everything went well, Papa and Mr. Morrison got home without any trouble.

Multiple Choice: Write ABCD in the space for the best answer.
1. _____ How many families still refused to shop at Wallace's store?
A. 10
B. 20
C. 7
D. 15

2. _____ When did Papa, Stacey, and Mr. Morrison leave for Vicksburg?
A. Wednesday
B. Monday
C. Saturday
D. Thursday

3. _____ Papa had a _____ and _____.
A. broken leg
B. shot to the head
C. both A and B
D. bad cough and head cold

4. _____ Mr. Granger and Mr. Montier raised what?
A. the cost of milk
B. the cost of flour
C. the cost of rice
D. the percentage of their share of the cotton harvest

Lesson 8
Write full sentences for this section:

1. Who shot at Papa and Mr. Morrison?
2. What did the Wallaces threaten the black families with?
3. Where did the attack on Papa happen?
4. When Mama said she was scared, what did Papa tell her?
5. Why did the two wheels of the wagon come off?
6. How did Papa's leg get broken?

(Who) _____
_____
_____
_____

(What)_____
_____
_____
_____

(Where)_____
_____
_____
_____

(When)_____
_____
_____
_____

(Why)_____
_____
_____
_____

(How)_____
_____
_____
_____

Fill in the Blanks: Write the vocabulary word that best completes the sentence.
Words: borrow   urgency   shroud   insecticide   scheme

1. "You think we should write Hammer and _____ some money?" Mama asked.
2. The bugs are getting so bad that the Logans are going to need _____ to get rid of them.
3. Mr. Morrison's voice was barely a whisper, but there was an _____ in it.
4. August heat swooped low over the land clinging like an invisible _____.
5. Mr. Granger wants to show David where he stands in the _____ of things.

True / False: Write T if statement is true; write F if it is false.
1. _____ Mama told Papa they had enough money to make the June payment and pay the taxes.
2. _____ Big Ma is thinking about shopping at the market in Strawberry.
3. _____ Mr. Morrison is going to look for another job because the Logan's have no money.
4. _____ Kaleb Wallace is one of those folks who can't do anything by himself.

Multiple Choice: Write ABCD in the space for the best answer.
1. _____ Where is Cassie's papa going to have his cotton ginned?
A. Strawberry
B. Vicksbury
C. Alabama
D. Missouri

2. _____ Who's pick-up truck did Mr. Morrison move off the road?
A. Mr. Granger's
B. Mr. Jameson's
C. Kaleb Wallace's
D. Mr. Bennett's

3. _____ Jeremy likes to sleep in a _____ during the summer.
A. tree
B. tent
C. little trailer
D. hammock

4. _____ Who did T.J. bring to the church the last day of the church revival?
A. Mr. Granger
B. Mr. Wallace
C. Mr. Bennett
D. R.W. and Melvin Simms

Lesson 9
Write full sentences for this section:

1. Who came from Chicago to bring Papa some money for the mortgage?
2. What need does Harlan Granger have for him to make trouble for the Logans?
3. Where are T.J. and the Simms brothers going?
4. When Mr. Morrison went to Strawberry to pay the mortgage, what did the bank give him?
5. Why does Stacey blame himself for his father's broken leg?
6. How is T.J. getting in trouble with his black neighbors?

(Who) _____
_____
_____
_____

(What)_____
_____
_____
_____

(Where)_____
_____
_____
_____

(When)_____
_____
_____
_____

(Why)_____
_____
_____
_____

(How)_____
_____
_____
_____

Fill in the Blanks: Write the vocabulary word that best completes the sentence.
Words: kerosene   compassion   responsibility   adamant   transfixed

1. Cassie could not show any _____ for T.J. after the way he treated them at the revival.
2. Stacey had always felt a _____ for T.J. that Cassie had never understood.
3. As the children neared the house the glow of the _____ lamp was shining in the window.
4. The children gazed _____ as the flames gobbled the cotton and traveled to the forest.
5. Christopher-John folded his arms across his chest and was _____ about staying home.

True / False: Write T if statement is true; write F if it is false.
1. _____ T.J.'s father is going to throw him out of the house if he doesn't come home one more night.
2. _____ R.W. and Melvin's intention is to rob Mr. Barnett's mercantile store.
3. _____ Both Mr. and Mrs. Barnett died from the attack at the store.
4. _____ Mr. Granger was so worried about the fire he stopped everyone to help.

Multiple Choice: Write ABCD in the space for the best answer.
1. _____ Who was looking for help from Stacey?
A. T.J.
B. R.W.
C. Melvin
D. Jeremy

2. _____ What did T.J. want from Stacey?
A. to give him some money
B. to help him get home
C. to help him runaway from home
D. to give him some food

3._____ Who tried to stop the attack on the Avery family?
A. Mr. Williams
B. the Simms brothers
C. Mr. Jamison and the sheriff
D. Mr. Morrison

4. _____ Who else do the attackers want to hang?
A. Mr. Morrison
B. David Logan
C. Stacey
D. both A and B

Lesson 10
Write full sentences for this section:

1. Who beat up T.J.?
2. What happened at the robbery?
3. Where did Mama tell Papa to get help from?
4. When did the night raiders come to the Avery's place?
5. Why did the Simms brothers beat-up T.J.?
6. How did David Logan stop the hanging?

(Who) _____
_____
_____
_____

(What)_____
_____
_____
_____

(Where)_____
_____
_____
_____

(When)_____
_____
_____
_____

(Why)_____
_____
_____
_____

(How)_____
_____
_____
_____

Answer Key

Lesson 1
Fill in the Blanks
1. meticulously
2. mortgage
3. monotonous
4. formidable
5. chiffonier
True and False
1. T
2. T
3. F
4. T
Multiple Choice
1. B
2. C
3. A
4. D
Who, What, Where, When, Why, and How
1. Little Man
2. the books are old, in very poor condition, and were given only to the black children
3. Smellings Creek
4. begins in October and ends in March
5. to pay the taxes and mortgage
6. 14 years

Lesson 2
Fill in the Blanks
1. humiliation
2. ignorant
3. outwit
4. oblivious
5. maneuvered
True and False
1. F
2. T
3. F
4. F
Multiple Choice
1. C
2. A
3. B
4. D
Who, What, Where, When, Why, and How
1. the Logan children
2. the axle broke and the engine was water logged
3. Strawberry
4. about two weeks
5. cause he just likes them
6. Mrs. Avery saw the white men gathering at Mr. Granger's house and sent her husband to tell them

Lesson 3
Fill in the Blanks
1. confirmed
2. trust
3. objections
4. cheating
5. faltered
True and False
1. T
2. F
3. F
4. F
Multiple Choice
1. D
2. A
3. B
4. C
Who, What, Where, When, Why, and How
1. Sam Tatum
2. sell her land to him
3. Vicksburg
4. T.J. slipped his notes on to Stacey's desk and Stacey got whipped for cheating
5. he called a white man a liar
6. he was a carpenter

Lesson 4
Fill in the Blanks
1. prevailed
2. regular
3. humiliated
4. insult
5. sullenly
True and False
1. F
2. T
3. T
4. T
Multiple Choice
1. B
2. A
3. D
4. C
Who, What, Where, When, Why, and How
1. Jeremy
2. a pearl handled handgun
3. at the lawyers office
4. Lillian Jean made trouble for her demanding an apology
5. he helps all the white folks first
6. no day in all of her life was as cruel as that one

Lesson 5
Fill in the Blanks
1. dumbfounded
2. bewildered
3. profitable
4. respect
5. opportunity
True and False
1. F
2. T
3. T
4. F
Multiple Choice
1. C
2. A
3. B
4. D
Who, What, Where, When, Why, and How
1. Papa's brother Hammer
2. knowledge of herbs and cures
3. on the old Soldiers Bridge
4. it is given with true respect and freedom
5. they believe their better because their white
6. some white people still did not see them as equals

Lesson 6
Fill in the Blanks
1. permanently
2. apprehensive
3. flounce
4. goaded
5. boycott
True and False
1. T
2. F
3. F
4. F
Multiple Choice
1. C
2. A
3. D
4. B
Who, What, Where, When, Why, and How
1. Mr. Morrison's parents and sisters
2. a man can not blame others for his own stupidity
3. Vicksburg
4. the Avery family
5. the coat was to big, made him look like a preacher, and all the other boys were laughing at him
6. Jeremy Simms brought gifts of nuts and a flute for Stacey

Lesson 7
Fill in the Blanks
1. prideful
2. forgiving
3. sensibly
4. gossip
5. threatened
True and False
1. F
2. T
3. T
4. T
Multiple Choice
1. B
2. D
3. C
4. A
Who, What, Where, When, Why, and How
1. T.J.
2. Cassie will tell all of Lillian Jean's friends all of her secrets
3. Wallace's Store
4. try studying
5. she is thirteen and Cassie is only nine
6. it's how you carry yourself and what you stand for

Lesson 8
Fill in the Blanks
1. enveloped
2. audible
3. unsympathetic
4. despairingly
5. confident
True and False
1. T
2. T
3. F
4. F
Multiple Choice
1. C
2. A
3. C
4. D
Who, What, Where, When, Why, and How
1. the Wallaces
2. if they don't pay their debts to him he is going to have the sheriff put them on the chain gang
3. on the rainy, muddy, dark road from Vicksburg
4. not yet, it's not time to get scared yet, their just talking, when they stop talking then it will be time
5. somebody loosened the bolts off the wagon wheels
6. the wagon rolled over his leg

Lesson 9
Fill in the Blanks
1. borrow
2. insecticide
3. urgency
4. shroud
5. scheme
True and False
1. F
2. T
3. F
4. T
Multiple Choice
1. B
2. C
3. A
4. D
Who, What, Where, When, Why, and How
1. Uncle Hammer
2. his need is to show them where they stand in the scheme of things and he wants their land
3. Barnett's Mercantile
4. a letter telling David that the whole mortgage was due and payable immediately
5. he was not strong enough to hold back Jack
6. he is running around with white boys and stealing from has neighbors

Lesson 10
Fill in the Blanks
1. compassion
2. responsibility
3. kerosene
4. transfixed
5. adamant
True and False
1. T
2. T
3. F
4. T
Multiple Choice
1. A
2. B
3. C
4. D
Who, What, Where, When, Why, and How
1. R.W. and Melvin Simms
2. R.W. hit Mr. Barnett on the head with an axe, Mrs. Barnett was pushed against a stove and hit her head
3. Harlan Granger
4. right after Stacey took T.J. home and was leaving
5. he wanted to tell someone what happened at Mr. Barnett's store
6. he started the fire so the men would have to stop the fire

CPSIA information can be obtained at www.ICGtesting.com
Printed in the USA
BVOW04s1140160815

413542BV00015B/273/P